Beyond Humpty Dumpty

Recovery Reflections on the
Seasons of Our Lives

Kenneth E. Ferber

Introduction

The phrase "cracked pot" has resonated deep within me for many years for its artistic, professional, and recovery applications. There is a curse in being cracked or broken, as in a "nonfunctioning" person or piece of pottery. Yet there is this life-giving spiritual insight: one of the powerful ways the light shines out of anyone is through their cracks, their weaknesses, their defects. It is when we are weak and humble, getting out of God's way, that the illuminating Spirit in us radiates outwardly, healing and transforming us and others.

My dysfunctional "cracked" side grew out of family conflict, abuse issues, and my own acting out, in addition to medication of pain through use of drugs and alcohol in my teen and adult years. It took me a long time to hit bottom. I was talented and successful as a musician, artist, husband, father, church planter, and parish pastor. Most things I undertook were blessed; they grew and multiplied for decades, until they all came tumbling down. I suffered the life-changing consequences of my actions and thereby began a true road to recovery.

It has been in my recovery over the years that a growing life theme became clear and very real to me. This is a powerful spiritual theme, but sadly, one that is often overlooked in our religious world where having more is taken as a blessing by God; and not being healed—not being "perfect"—is often seen as an absence of that blessing, or worse, as a sign of not being saved.

It took a near-death experience in 2006 for me to get to the place where I could admit, for the first time, that I was an alcoholic and my life had become unmanageable. It was also from this ordeal of deep brokenness and humility that the theme of these reflections was not simply scratched at as it had been for years through sermons and teachings in churches and conferences, but became a daily, living reality and source of strength.

This truth is simple and can be introduced with reference to the Humpty Dumpty nursery rhyme. Whatever we call our Higher Power or God or some king or queen with power greater than ourselves, the rhyme rings true: "All the king's horses and all the king's men couldn't put Humpty together again." Whatever our spirituality names as its source of being, that power is not interested in simply putting us back together again if we are broken. No, that power, in the daily miracle of miracles, is the great recycler! That power not only wants to take all the broken pieces of our lives that we are willing and able to surrender, but also wants to recycle those very pieces and make a new creation—one that could not exist if it had never been broken—a brand-new creation!

This is the daily miracle of recovery, and it is available to all. We are never finished, but are always in the growing process. Our Higher Power's grace, freely given each day, allows us to live a thankful life of gratitude despite our worst tragedies. We are perfectly flawed. It is only when we see our brokenness and inability to heal ourselves that we are infused with power outside ourselves. That power transforms us, sometimes quickly, sometimes slowly, but always surely.

The miracle of recovery that shines through the reflections in this book teaches us that in true transformation we will never be what we once were during our best years, but we can be better than we've ever been, despite our worst years!

This is the underlying theme of these readings as played out in my life of recovery and in the lives of hundreds of others who have shined their light on me, through me, and out to you. My desire for the reader of these words is the expression we often used during my seminary years: "May the truths of these pages be read, marked, learned, and inwardly digested" for the best growth possible. This is my prayer.

Photography

All photographs were taken by the author near his home on the Beaver Island Trail and along the Mississippi River in St. Cloud, Minnesota.

SPRING

New Life from Near Death

Steps 1–3: Give Up
(Page 13)

+ + + + +

SUMMER

The Healing Sunshine of Summer

Steps 4-7: Clean Up
(Page 87)

AUTUMN

Getting Ready For Wintry Times

Steps 8-9: Make Up
(Page 153)

+ + + + +

WINTER

Enjoying It By Getting Out Into It

Steps 10-12: Keep Up
(Page 193)

Spring

*Sitting quietly, doing nothing,
Spring comes, and the grass
grows by itself.*

—The Gospel According To Zen

Steps 1–3: Give Up

*A new life. A new beginning. The
chilling, destructive and near-deadly snows
have thawed, and there is spring. There is
another chance. There is new life!*

Step 1

We admitted we were powerless over alcohol, and our lives had become unmanageable.

Theme: Honesty

I give up the illusions that I control the alcoholic, that I am sane, and that I can manage my life alone. I cannot.

Switching Chairs on the Titanic

I received that "recovery-contentment" blessing at this morning's AA meeting. I think that for many years I was searching in churches for the best of what I have found in AA: not only genuine and transparent people who are honest, open, and willing to be available, but also a nonjudgmental atmosphere where concerns and topics can be shared in a safe environment. Each member can choose to add his or her own experience and wisdom. Occasionally I have found such an environment in a church, but I always find it at the AA meetings I attend.

Because today's speaker did not show up, the topic was just thrown out by a first time visitor who was also new in recovery: "What are your greatest struggles with alcohol?" As the topic circled the group a theme emerged: "I don't have a drinking or drugging problem—I have a *living problem*." To put it another way: "Take away the drugs and alcohol and I still have trouble living this life, this painful life that I was trying to escape through my use."

Another person talked about feeling better smoking weed since he was no longer drinking himself into blackouts, but he came to understand the reality of this "stinking thinking." Another member chimed in, saying, "Yeah, it's like my dad who is a recovering alcoholic says about going from alcohol to another drug, 'It's like switching chairs on the Titanic, the ship is still going down!'" Then, to show how this thinking turns into classic rationalization, the next member says, "Yeah—when you talked about the ship still going down, I'm thinking to myself, "'But weren't there a bunch of survivors from the Titanic?'" I thought, "Wow, cunning, baffling, and powerful!"

Another member talked about the diminishing quality of his sobriety. He is still very active and goes to a number of meetings a week, but that inner joy and connection with his Higher Power has changed. Someone else said, "When I was first in recovery, I wrote in lipstick on my bathroom mirror, *the problem is you!*" She was speaking of her living problem, not just her addiction problem. She got tired of wiping it off all the time, so she stenciled it permanently above the mirror.

From these personal testimonies a host of introspective questions rise up in my mind and heart, especially since I don't have the desire to drink any more. "How is my Higher Power involved in my living problem?" "What have I learned from my past living problems?" "How might I be switching chairs on the Titanic by moving from alcohol to something else in my life that keeps me from healing and growing in my recovery?" "How do I continue to be honest, open, willing, and transparent, getting rid of the secrets in my life that cannot only cause deep hurt and pain to me and others, but can also destroy years of work? Am I in danger of falling from grace once again and the recovery place I am at now?"

But I do not have to worry or let any of these questions overwhelm me. My Higher Power permeates all these questions with forgiveness, grace, strength, and mercies that truly are new every morning. This is "the wisdom to know the difference."*

Higher Power, continue to grant me that life-changing wisdom, saving me from myself.

---

*The Serenity Prayer is not only spoken at the beginning of most AA meetings around the world but it is also a powerful tool to help anyone cope with their daily living. Although the first few sentences are what is spoken at meetings, I added the prayer in its entirety (see following page) from Reinhold Niebuhr. What is spoken as meetings begin is *God grant me the Serenity to accept the things I cannot change, Courage to change the things I can, and the Wisdom to know the difference.* This is slightly different from the original.

The Serenity Prayer

By Reinhold Niebuhr (1892-1971)
Complete Unabridged, Original Version

God, give us grace to accept with Serenity the things that cannot be changed, Courage to change the things which should be changed, and the Wisdom to distinguish the one from the other. Living one day at a time, enjoying one moment at a time, accepting hardship as a pathway to peace. Taking, as Jesus did, this sinful world as it is, not as I would have it. Trusting that You will make all things right if I surrender to Your will, so that I may be reasonably happy in this life and supremely happy with You forever in the next. + Amen.

Back in Fifteen Minutes!

She's from New York, but moved out to Minnesota a few years ago to begin to recover and raise her teenage son. We ran into each other at the large coffee pot before the meeting. She was wearing the neatest wide-brimmed straw hat, calling it "my country-girl look." She is a great addition and blessing to our Wednesday 10:00 a.m. AA group--colorful, unpredictable, not afraid to share her vulnerability or hesitant to ask if anybody needs a little time before we begin. Last Wednesday she shared with the group a recent embarrassing public incident that almost landed her in jail but turned out for the best. The story initially made her look weak and powerless, but upon reflection, it empowered her and us. The power wasn't coming from her, but from her Higher Power.

This week she shared a story titled "Back in Fifteen Minutes." I asked her after the meeting if I could use it in my writing and she agreed. Our meeting topic was humility in our recovery. She told us that in the midst of the darkest period of her addiction she owned and operated a shop in New York City. She would often find herself hiding beneath the table in her shop, not wanting to see or speak to anyone. She regularly locked her shop and put a sign on the front door "Back in Fifteen Minutes." She would escape to the bar just down the street, exceeding her fifteen-minute limit by hours, if not days. She said, "I would always keep putting that sign on the front door. Back in fifteen minutes—back in fifteen minutes—back in fifteen minutes. That's how I lived my life!"

Wow! That phrase slipped beneath my defenses and I pondered my own "back in fifteen minutes" signs I frequently post. Think of those dark times of escape, hiding, running, avoiding, stuffing, burying, and so much more, cavernous depths of mere existence, on the edge, teetering, almost gone. Places where we could have gone either way, where we could have slipped into oblivion.

It is empowering to see my friend's smile, encouraging words, and bright colors almost every week now. Her brutal honesty and self-effacement strip away much of the darkness I find myself still wanting to hide in, under the table with others walking all around me. She is refreshing, even on her fragile days when she needs more time—perhaps especially then.

———————————

A simple guide to the first three Steps:

Step 1: I Can't
Step 2: He Can
Step 3: I Think I'll Let Him

———————————

Shame and Enslavement

I was surprisingly empowered this morning by leading a group that talked about guilt and shame and the difference between the two. A big part of healing from shame is to learn the difference between "I made a mistake" and "I *am* a mistake." One of the handouts regarding shame contains a story entitled "The Duck."

There's the oft-used wise saying: "When the student is ready, the master appears." I could also say that when the presenter needs an illustration the email appears. It was years ago that I first received the very same handout she gave me today, but I had forgotten about it. Just when I needed it for my own healing and to assist others in the same, just when I needed it to remind myself and others of our Higher Power's unconditional love, it appeared. Perfect timing.

The Duck

Author Unknown

There was a little boy visiting his grandparents on their farm. He was given a slingshot to play with out in the woods. He practiced in the woods, but he could never hit the target. Getting a little discouraged, he headed back for dinner. As he was walking back he saw

Grandma's pet duck. Just out of impulse, he let the slingshot fly, hit the duck square in the head and killed it. He was shocked and grieved!

In a panic, he hid the dead duck in the wood pile, only to see his sister watching! Sally had seen it all, but she said nothing. After lunch the next day Grandma said, "Sally, let's wash the dishes," but Sally said, "Grandma, Johnny told me he wanted to help in the kitchen." Then she whispered to him, "Remember the duck?" So Johnny did the dishes.

Later that day, Grandpa asked if the children wanted to go fishing and Grandma said, "I'm sorry, but I need Sally to help make supper." Sally just smiled and said, "Well that's all right, because Johnny told me he wanted to help." Then she whispered again, "Remember the duck?" So Sally went fishing and Johnny stayed to help. After several days of Johnny doing both his chores and Sally's, he finally couldn't stand it any longer. He came to Grandma and confessed that he had killed the duck.

Grandma knelt down, gave him a hug and said, "Sweetheart, I know. You see, I was standing at the window and I saw the whole thing, but because I love you, I forgave you. I was just wondering how long you would let Sally make a slave of you."

A Breakdown That Causes A Breakthrough

A newcomer at today's meeting asked me to lunch. I had just enough time to do so before my second meeting at 1:30 p.m. It had been an extremely heavy, emotionally draining first meeting on Step 2 that caused deep and painful father-child relationships to surface within me. Almost everyone was shedding silent tears at some point around the table.

While driving to lunch two blocks away, the noon speaker on NPR had an interesting theme for his speech that seemed so like recovery: "The Breakdown that Caused a Breakthrough." I didn't catch much of it, but the speaker was talking about all the major breakdowns in history, like wars, massacres, and religious persecutions, that were followed by major breakthroughs, such as peace accords, growing race relationships, and much more!

This, for me, is the heart of true recovery: a major breakthrough because of a major breakdown. How could all of us who have experienced slow, steady transformations over the days, months, and years have come to this point of breakthrough without a breakdown? Such derailments contribute to the breakdown of our often defiant self-destructive wills, laying a foundation receptive to the Spirit's reconstruction program. The fruit of this self-destruction can lead to true humility and surrender, and to letting God, our Higher Power, *be God* in our lives.

Perhaps there would have been another way for my Higher Power to get my attention, changing my heart and giving me back a life beyond my expectations, but I can't think of what that would have been. I am beyond thankful for the Spirit's powerful direction in my life, and in so many other lives around me, preparing us for this new journey—even if it takes a breakdown to get a breakthrough.

Stick Around Until the
Miracle Happens

The topic at our meeting this morning was "AA phrases that are helpful and healing for our ongoing sobriety." I had forgotten one that resurfaced today and was worth getting out of bed for: *Stick around until the miracle happens*, which reminds us of what happens when we *keep coming back,* another well-worn favorite.

My favorite phrase has always been *We will love you until you learn to love yourself;* this expresses the best of sobriety through an active recovery program. During the sharing, another member talked about how lonely he was when he went to bars, saying, "I didn't know a damn soul!" This made me think of a destructive parallel phrase: "I only knew damned souls when I was using." This is not a judgmental statement. Rather, many souls who have hit bottom without surrendering or giving up *feel like damned souls*, and misery loves company.

There are those also who feel unworthy, or that no one loves them, including a supposedly loving God. The concept of an unconditional Higher Power that accepts them *completely*, just where they are, is unbelievable. This is why it is so empowering to have an in-the-trenches experience of receiving that kind of love. When we live out our program among those feeling like outcasts and not knowing what to believe, we become "Jesus with skin on him" to those who have lost hope and have little or no power.

This miracle also happened today during our meeting. A man had been a prominent member, active in service work, rarely missing a meeting. His bold sharing seemed to come from the heart and was filled with perfect recovery statements, all driven home with strong emphasis. He was also a veteran who spoke to other veterans. He had been absent from our meetings for some time but came back today and said he had hurt a lot of people due to his using while he pretended to be clean and sober. He had only been clean for four days. It was quiet in the room.

His confession was powerful and humbling, and all present welcomed him back with open arms. Why was that? Because we had all been there! All of us knew about the hypocrisy of the disease in one way or another, presenting our Mr. Hyde side while living in the shadows as Dr. Jekyll. I knew it all too well. I was the picture of spiritual health as a well-known pastor of a growing and diverse church, welcoming outcasts and those in recovery, even preaching recovery words and concepts while I was using and carrying on. I was living a lie while preaching and living out publicly just the opposite.

There is another reason why this former hypocritical member, now the "prodigal returned," was believable and true: he checked himself back into treatment almost two months ago. He's been working his program daily and is currently sharing his testimony of his relapse at Speakers' Meetings, weekly recovery groups, and more. "The proof *is* in the pudding." "Your talk talks, and your walk talks, but your walk talks *louder* than your talk talks!" Not unlike the phrase "People would rather *see* a sermon than hear one any day."

What an *awesome* Higher Power we have, however you experience that power. My experience has been that this Power never stops reaching out in unconditional love, loving to the end, and then loving some more. I have stuck around; I have kept coming back. The miracle has happened and continues to happen. I have been loved, even as I am learning to love myself. I am now growing in my ability to pass that love on to others, putting a little skin on my Higher Power for them to see.

Step 2

Came to believe that a Power greater than ourselves could restore us to sanity

Theme: Hope

I ran everywhere but to God! There was only one direction I hadn't run, and that was toward the God of my understanding, Beginning with G.O.D.

GOOD ORDERLY DIRECTION.

Fake It (Faith it) Till You Make It!

The recovery phrase "fake it till you make it" keeps bouncing around in my head from recovery literature and meetings. I know exactly what this refers to, and practicing this phrase has helped me in my recovery, but I struggle with the language of the phrase. It reminds me of a time when I did just "fake it" without "making it" as I isolated myself, using, misusing, and abusing my drug of choice.

The phrase "Build the form and let your Higher Power fill it" is a better fit for me. It is a phrase that has moved beyond "wet cement" and into the concrete phase, to continue the metaphor of sidewalk construction. When I was directly involved with building a large church, I spent many days watching the workers create new sidewalks by first building two-by-four frames, then waiting for the cement truck to come and fill those forms. This is a helpful analogy for me in daily living.

I know I am powerless. In my understanding, this means I can only build the form, believing that my powerful Higher-Power-Cement-Truck will come and fill it, even though that process can take a long time. I can "faith it till I make it." I read recently about a European country that is building a whole set of railroad tracks over the Alps, even though it could be years, if ever, before train service even comes to that area. They built it in faith, believing it would come, not unlike the faith of Ray Kinsella in the movie *Field of Dreams* who heard the haunting voice say, "If you build it, he will come!" He built it and his father came. There was deep healing in their relationship.

I am building it. My Higher Power comes daily, often through other people, and fills the form. Very often it is a completely different result than I expected. It's like the chorus of the song, "You can't always get what you want, but if you try some time, you just might find, you get what you need." What I have received is so much more than what I have needed.

In recovery, I have been given power, strength, energy, enthusiasm and peace as a result of the twelve-step program, living out the 12 Promises* in my life. If I did not have that "spiritual cement truck" to fill the forms I build daily, I believe there would be nothing of lasting or eternal value.

Peace and hope as we are empowered to build the form, remembering that "Faith is the substance of things hoped for, the evidence of things not seen."
Hebrews 11:1

The Spiritual Steps of the Program - 2,3,11

I am born alone. I die alone. I spend my life drawing near to others so I will not be alone, yet catching glimpses of the DIVINE that lives in and through me, helping me believe I am never alone...

Can this be true?

*The 12 Promises of AA

If we are painstaking about this phase of our development, we will be amazed before we are halfway through…

1. We are going to know a new freedom and a new happiness.

2. We will not regret the past nor wish to shut the door on it.

3. We will comprehend the word *serenity*.

4. We will know peace.

5. No matter how far down the scale we have gone, we will see how our experience can benefit others.

6. That feeling of uselessness and self-pity will disappear.

7. We will lose interest in selfish things and gain interest in our fellows.

8. Self-seeking will slip away.

9. Our whole attitude and outlook upon life will change.

10. Fear of people and of economic insecurity will leave us.

11. We will intuitively know how to handle situations which used to baffle us.

12. We will suddenly realize that God is doing for us what we could not do for ourselves.

Are these extravagant promises? We think not. They are being fulfilled among us, sometimes quickly, sometimes slowly. They will always materialize if we work for them.

From *The Big Book of Alcoholics Anonymous, Fourth* Edition, pp. 83-84. Copyright © AA World Services, Inc. (Reprinted with permission)

Incredible Gifts from
Incredible Disasters

Many years ago I was taken to the next level in my understanding of God when reading how the life of Joni Erickson Tada was forever changed by a tragic diving accident that left her a quadriplegic.

What I remember most was that she had never known she possessed amazing gifts as an artist and musician until her accident and her extremely long, arduous rehabilitation period. For most people, to go from being an active, athletic person to a lifelong quadriplegic would be one of the greatest setbacks possible. Joni would never again be the way she had been. God had a different plan. Only through adversity and extreme disaster could His best gifts shine through this amazing vessel and conduit of His light.

There are many other avenues Joni could have gone, many of them negative and self-destructive, but she chose to embrace her crisis, allowing the Spirit to recycle her life. This is the theme of my life, this book, my art, and so many walking wounded human beings that have become wounded healers. God made a new creation in Joni, something only possible because of the deep physical, emotional, mental, and spiritual pain she went through. She learned not only how to survive from it but to miraculously *thrive* through it.

I am inspired and humbled by the fact that God did not "heal" her physically, though He could have and still can if He so wills. It was not because she did not have enough faith, as we often hear with bad theology and misunderstanding of the way God's Spirit works today. You can debate whether God allowed or caused the accident, as believers have been doing for millennia. God could have prevented this accident but chose not to. **His inaction was the power of His greatest action in Joni's life,** and often in our recovery. Hmmm—kind of reminds me of what happened to my Higher Power on the cross.

There can be peace and healing through crisis. Sometimes this may be the only way we can be healed, discovering gifts we never knew we had!

A diving accident in 1967 left Mrs. Tada a quadriplegic in a wheelchair, unable to use her hands. After two years of rehabilitation, Joni reentered the community with new skills and a fresh determination to help others in similar situations. "My church made a huge difference in my family's life as they demonstrated the love of God in practical ways," says Joni. Mrs. Tada wrote of her experiences in her international bestselling biography, Joni. *Her name is now recognized in countries around the world following the distribution in many languages of her biography and the full-length feature film* Joni. *She has personally visited over 41 countries.*

Overheard in an Orchard

Said the Robin to the Sparrow:
"I should really like to know
Why these anxious human beings
Rush about and worry so?"

Said the Sparrow to the Robin:
"Friend, I think that it must be
That they have no Heavenly Father
Such as cares for you and me."

―――――――――

—Elizabeth Cheney

―――――――――

Is Being Still Actually Possible?

Asking questions to ascertain truth.

What does it mean to be *still?* The Psalmist writes: *Be still and know that I AM God* (46:10). In trying to better understand stillness, a few key phrases leap into my mind from my heart:

Don't just do something; stand there.

Be here; be now. Be in the moment.
Be centered. Be fully present.

There was a time, thanks to my sister and brother-in-law, when I was blessed to live in the Hawaiian Islands for a few years. There I practiced vegetarianism, immersing myself in Eastern mysticism, meditation, and exercise, including various forms of yoga with my own instructor. I experienced a deep mellowness and greater control of my mind and thoughts. Was that "being still"? This desired state of achievement certainly goes beyond the physical, mental, and emotional, but is it mostly spiritual? If you have the spiritual part, do the others fall into place? Is it possible to separate the spiritual from the mental, emotional, and physical aspects of our daily living? Is it possible that *all* things are spiritual? Could it be that all things are sacred, but we have a tendency to separate them into different categories, making some dominate while others almost disappear?

This questioning and searching for meaning in stillness surfaced during one of my recovery readings, and was further distilled at my Wednesday AA meeting. The most appealing phrase of this reflection was: "it was from the stillness that the power seemed to arise to deal with the crisis" (Mark Nepo, *The Book of Awakening*). If this is true, why don't I practice it more often? Do I not believe it? Is the Spirit willing but the flesh weak? Am I just too busy? As the saying goes, "If you are too busy to take times for spirituality (being still) then you are *too busy!*" If so, perhaps I should ask myself "Why am I so busy?" Is it for money, esteem, survival, fear of drinking, using, relapsing, or all of the above?

If I know deep down that practicing stillness really works, adding a peace and joy and contentment in my life that has long since faded, what's the problem with "just doing it?" Is it that dark side of human nature? I will speak only for myself here, but I've seen, felt, and struggled with that self-destructive part that lies in wait within, begging to be in charge—to be God! I have found when embracing this ever-encroaching nature, I am led to a place of unmanageability and will eventually find myself out of control. Even if I could be God, or a god, I could not sustain it with my ever-present always-changing weak human nature. I need a power greater than myself for strength and ongoing healing.

Our weekly AA group speaker did not show up and we moved to Plan B, which was this very reading. The question circled the table regarding how each one present practiced what they understood stillness to be in their lives. The majority of comments from the twenty-four members present were something like those of the NFL coach with a struggling team when asked about making the playoffs last year: "Stillness? Are you kidding me?" "Stillness? Are you *kidding* me? *Stillness*? There was a consensus: most of the group expressed an extreme lack of personal stillness and peace.

My personal stillness came in hitting bottom; truly surrendering; spending the last eighteen months of sobriety in weekly meetings; attending therapy, sponsor, and sponsee meetings; working with others in recovery; and pursuing a growing, honest relationship with my Higher Power. What else is there, short of an immediate miraculous transformation? God certainly can and has worked that way, but getting zapped is not usually exercised by the Divine. It is more often achieved one day at a time.

When push comes to shove and the handwriting is on the wall, clearly written in large letters, I know it's time to seek stillness. I have experienced far too much miraculous intervention in my life not to know how to achieve a greater stillness. The best answer and action is not to beat up on myself, but realize how I am progressing in my recovery. I need to continue doing more of what I know, staying away from cross-addictions, and living out the 12 Steps of Alcoholics Anonymous. I can use Steps 2, 3 and 11 to continue improving my conscious contact with God, praying for a growing understanding of His will and His power to daily carry that out.

It's a simple program, but it is not easy. I know through these steps I will achieve a greater stillness in my life, and thereby a stillness that seeps into the lives of others around me.

"God, help me do what You have already taught me, and keep me from sabotaging your grace in my life. Give me a continued desire to desire it."

Fireproofed!

I heard a poem this morning entitled "The Bible Belt" that made me give thanks for the spiritual freedom I have in AA. My God is a God of unconditional love, loving me completely where I'm at and graciously moving me to where He wants me to be. He is not how others think I should understand God when they preach at me that "this is the truth!" Some have even told me that I need to be fireproofed! Fireproofed, I thought, for what? "Against the FIRES OF HELL!"

Oh, I see—your god, not my God, fireproofs you against the fires of Hell! Hmmmmmm, quite a choice. Let's see, "Believe in me or go straight to hell! Believe in me or spend eternity in torment in the undying flames." Wow! What a god! A god that would make me into Asbestos Boy!

The problem with this understanding is that since we are powerless, having *no power*, we'd all be damned by this brand of spirituality, which puts more emphasis on what we have to do than what our gracious, loving God has already done.

There are also some pastors and priests in recovery who feel many in AA water down the truth with their Higher Power language. They have their *Big Book* and *BIG BOOK* meetings, combining the bible of AA, *The Big Book*, with the Holy Bible. But that's OK. As one of my recovery friends likes to say: "Whatever works for their recovery."

I do understand this thinking, as I used to be one of those who felt others were watering down the message. Then I began to work as a chaplain in recovery centers with men and women in recovery. I found just the opposite—many had been spiritually abused and shamed by the church as well as by their own family members with phrases like "If you just believed, you wouldn't drink!" "If you just had enough faith, you wouldn't use drugs!" I found that when I didn't shove God or Jesus or the Spirit down people's throats, they were empowered to choose, and many returned to the God of their upbringing, or were open to observing and learning from their peers who had faith.

I have also found ignorance of recovery principles among professionals, where I used to be, but I thank God for a growing consciousness among many who see those who were the walking dead now living lives of purpose and hope and helping others do the same. Many of them realized that all their professional practices did not change others the way the simple 12-step program truly did, and often working in tandem, each complementing the other. The proof is in the pudding!

Thank God for Bill W. and Dr. Bob, the founders of AA, and for all the struggles they went through with God's guidance over seventy-five years ago, to get us to the place we are today. They knew that God, as we understand God, is all-powerful. They knew that He can take care of Himself. He has simply said, "Seek and you will find." I like that. All who seek God will find God because He has promised it. He is a God of love and mercy and grace who freely gives us love and mercy and grace, when we have none, even when we are running away—again.

Yes, we are free to believe in a fireproofing god, as well as the One who went through the God-forsaken fires of hell for us, or, none of the above.

A friend and former Roman Catholic priest used to say in his talks about sexuality with college students: "God is a gentle lover; He does not rape us, or force Himself on us. He waits, He is patient. His love empowers us—often overpowers us—and draws us to Himself, ever closer all the time."

Disagreeing Agreeably

Recovery is a spiritual program and a process. If we do not admit that we have a problem and call upon a power greater than ourselves, we will eventually relapse and die—this is the end result of our disease—and that's just the way it is. But just because it's a spiritual program does not mean we have to accept hook, line, and sinker what people around us believe. We have the Spirit in us to help us discern what is true for us—what we can believe at this time and what we cannot. We will be involved in this evolution our whole lives. We stay open each day in prayer, asking God to teach us what we need to know and to stay open to receive it, as Step 11 states so well:

We sought through prayer and meditation to improve our conscious contact with God, as we understood Him, praying only for knowledge of His will for us and the power to carry that out.

Having read through one of the popular (non-AA sanctioned) recovery reflection books twice in two years, I have learned much and work on applying it to my life. I also continue to learn what I do not believe, or what does not work spiritually for me. A lot of religious stuff is thrown at me from that book, as well as from one religious fanatic at my home meeting. As I bristle at his fanaticism and what I perceive as his close-mindedness, I can hear the words of my treatment counselor echoing in my brain: "We alcoholics are fiercely independent and often have trouble with authority figures!" Who, me?

So keep it simple. You will read this phrase more than once in this book and hear it frequently at AA meetings:

It's a simple program, but it's not an easy program.

As the Big Book states, those who have the hardest time in recovery are "too smart, too religious, and too rich." I can't fully comment on the rich part, but I certainly have fit the too-religious category, and strongly resemble the too-smart department, thinking too much, and sometimes guilty of "analysis paralysis"!

Today's reading in *Twenty-Four Hours A Day* began with what I believe to be a false statement as I continue to understand my disease of alcoholism in more practical ways which apply directly to my life and faith:

AA Thought for the Day - March 9

If we had absolute faith in the power of God to keep us from drinking and if we turned our drink problem entirely over to God without reservations, we wouldn't have to do anything more about it. We'd be free from drink once and for all. But since our faith is apt to be weak, we have to strengthen and build up this faith.....

So is this an incurable disease or not? Is this disease based upon our genetic makeup, or, do we just need a little more faith to be able to drink socially? If I just have enough faith will my life then be normal? Would I be cured? After years of active recovery I feel and believe that I am free from drink once and for all, though I don't let my guard down. I try to live like Martin Luther once wrote: "Live as if everything depended on you, and pray as if everything depended on God."

There will always be bad theology as well as wolves in sheep's clothing in our recovery world, which is why we are given growing discernment and wisdom through our recovery program. This truth came home to me last night as I watched a television evangelist for just one minute while surfing through the channels. In his best preaching tone he said, "We got that bad medical report that said, 'Things don't look good.' But we have *another report from God*, and if we have enough faith we will be healed!" Way to blame the victim! That way the faith healer is always let off the hook if the sick one is not healed, because, well, "he just didn't have enough faith."

Last time I checked *all* of the Saints—those in the Bible with the greatest faith, the kind that moved mountains—are dead! In fact, one of the most beautiful spiritual truths for me is that death can be "the ultimate healing," going home, being complete, translated:

Enoch walked with God; then he was no more, because God took him away. Genesis 5:24

The saddest part of this bad theology is that it misrepresents one of my strongest core beliefs: *My alcoholism has become a precious gift to me from my Higher Power.* That Power has miraculously worked through my disease and given me an amazing new life that I could never experience without being blessed with this disease. I don't want to be "cured" of that. I don't want faith to lead me to overlook all that I've been given and how I've continued to grow within my recovery. I want to pass it on to others for their continued growth and healing. I do not want to be cured and be able to drink normally.

I am thankful for all my readings, teaching me more deeply about my own spirituality, not what others think I should believe. My own personal faith and discernment consist of growing slowly but steadily in my recovery.

"Take what works, and leave the rest."

Daily Getting Into the Wheelbarrow

Letting Go and Letting God

There is a story about a guy who accidentally drives his car over the edge of a cliff. As the car is falling to its destruction he manages to open the door, leap out, and cling to a rocky ledge, watching his car burst into flames as it crashes to earth below. Barely hanging on, slipping and slowly losing his grip, he cries out to God, "Help! Save me!" His cries are muffled by a loud, clear voice, "Let go and I'll catch you!" He can't believe it! The last thing he wants to do is let go and experience the same fate as his car. He keeps crying, and keeps hearing God's voice, "Let go, and I'll catch you!" The man then cries out, "Is there anyone else up there?"

"Letting go and letting God." Easy to say, difficult to do. It reminds me of another story that helped take me to the next level in what it means to walk the talk, practice what I preach and live out my faith in a greater way each day.

A world-class tightrope walker announces that he's going to stretch a steel cable from the American to the Canadian side of Niagara Falls and walk across it. Thousands of people gather at the Falls. The acrobat, mounting the cable, yells out to the crowd, "How many of you believe I can walk across and back safely?" They all yell out, "We believe you can do it! We have faith in you!"

The tightrope walker goes across and comes back safely. The crowd cheers wildly. He does the same, pushing a wheelbarrow across and back, with the mist rising up perilously, as the crowd roars more loudly in approval. Then he yells to the crowd, "I want to walk across again pushing and balancing this wheelbarrow! You all believe I can do it! You all have faith in me that I can accomplish this great feat, but I have a more important question for all of you. Which one of you is going to be the first to get *into* the wheelbarrow?"

It's easy to talk the talk, but not so easy to walk the talk. It's easy to say it, but we are called to "get in the wheelbarrow," putting our faith and our lives in the hands of our Higher Power. We are called to let that Power truly have control over our life and death and our life after life! The good news is that we are powerless to do that, but our Higher Power has all power and gives us the strength and desire to daily get into the wheelbarrow, placing ourselves into His hands that hold us, or at least that *want* to hold us.

I have often wanted to add to this special story of faith. When the tightrope walker cries out to the crowd asking who will be the first to get into the wheelbarrow, I envision a child's hand shooting up into the air and hearing a voice saying "I will!" A little girl comes running to the tightrope walker and jumps into the wheelbarrow! I'm not sure where her parents are, but perhaps they were right there, seeing her childlike faith and encouraging her. One of my favorite phrases is "Growing up to be a child." Not a childish faith, but a childlike faith that is willing to jump into the wheelbarrow simply because she believes in the one pushing it!

We all know and love the poem "Footprints" because of the part that speaks to a time when we had no power, believing it was then that God carried us. How are these car-crash and Niagara Falls stories any different? Whether we are completely helpless, hanging on by a thread, or when we need to traverse a huge tight rope in our lives, it all begins with using the power we're given to let go and let God carry us.

Your talk talks,
And your walk talks,
But your walk talks
Louder than your talk talks.

Surrender to Time

What does the phrase *surrender to time* really mean? It came from my daily reflection reading and has taken days to sink into my spiritual understanding. I know it is a critical piece of my transformational puzzle. It began germinating when I publicly read it a second time during a topical meeting I led on "Acceptance and Contentment-- Living Simply and Joyfully in the Present."

On my *bad days* I am obsessed by time and the myriad of thoughts and questions it produces in me: How do I live with contentment and joy in the present if I am held hostage by time? No matter how hard I wrestle with time, twenty-four-seven, I will never win. I will not beat it, defeat it, or have more hours in the day than anyone else has. I am a slave to time; I can *never* get all the things I want done. I am held prisoner in dreary loneliness that no amount of time can fill. I am powerless over time, and it is true that "time marches on" and "time waits for no one; No! Not even you!"

What adds fuel to this fire is the haunting thought about a time when I run out of time—death, when time is no more; yet, death, when I am liberated from the bondage of time? Death, new life? Life after life? A place where there is no time? Or is it simply a cessation of existence as we become worm food, and enter the "long dirt nap"? What's it all about?

On my *good days*, which are slowly growing in my life of recovery, my fears are diminished. I am awakened to my Higher Power's presence as an experience of timelessness in the midst of ordinary days. I am privileged now and then to visit the outer courts of this new space and presence. It's like a "tractor beam" from "Star Trek," constantly pulling me closer, when I think of this sacred place; my head is instantly bypassed to my heart. It is a presence where glimpses and foretastes are experienced. I am convinced during these not-so-frequent epiphanies that I am not a human being having a timeless experience, but am instead a timeless being having a human experience.

I believe a relationship with a Higher Power is an experience in timelessness. A few synonyms for *timeless* are *spirituality, heaven, presence, contentment,* and even *simplicity.* This touches on the best of what I understand the Zen experience to be: "Chop wood, carry water," the total sacredness of the ordinary, the everyday, when we are given flowing time to swim in, to enjoy. These are blessed times when I am learning to tread water, allowing the current to carry me to yet another amazing place, using everything I have learned in my life. Nothing is wasted.

I surrender to time. I am powerless over it. Yet time can and does stop for me, and not only in the finality of my death. The hope for a place of timelessness is not simply "pie in the sky when I die." I am learning to enter those timeless holes each day during such simple, miraculous activities as reflection readings, meditation, prayer, going to meetings, fellowship, or just enjoying the day and my dog. When I do, there is a miracle of multiplication. I cannot document this in the theatre of the mind, but when I "let go and let God," being as present as possible in the sacred all around me, I feel I am given more time—I am able to get more done and go about my work with a rare contentment.

Martin Luther, when once asked what his plans for the following day were, answered: "Work, work, from early until late. In fact, I have so much to do that I shall spend the first three hours in prayer."

I surrender to the God of my understanding,
to be still and know that He blesses me
with time to grow and help others grow;
that He gives me glimpses of timelessness
in my everyday activities, and a hope
for such a place in eternity.

Grace, Works, Healing, Recovery

How good it is for me to think about grace. I easily forget about amazing grace that saved someone like me. To be saved means a lot of things to a lot of people; some even use it to make others feel like they are not accepted or loved by God because they don't believe the way they do. But "saved" also means "pulled from the wreckage," "snatched from the burning house," "rescued after going under for the last time" and so many other life-saving expressions. I have experienced this mysterious tough-love grace freely in my life; it not only brought me to my rock-bottom but also began my healing journey of recovery.

I am being changed by the grace of my Higher Power. It is helping me to believe there is no sin I can even imagine---let alone commit---that will cause me to be loved any less. I stop holding my breath when I remember again that there is *nothing* I can do to save myself other than what has already been done for me in that rescuing grace. People always want to add something to that grace, perhaps to feel like they are *doing* something, or to maintain some of their own power and control.

My professor at seminary came into the classroom one day and asked us, "What is it that will be in heaven for all eternity that man alone has done, placed there by his own hands, his own works?" We were baffled, having been taught well about grace and God's works in us, empowering us when we have no power. We were all silent, not wanting to sound heretical. He waited. Finally, in silence, he pointed to the center of each of his hands and said, "The only thing that will be in heaven because of man's works—because of *our works*—will be the holes from the nails in His hands. That is the only thing I can contribute."

---

*Amazing grace, how sweet the sound
that saved a wretch like me.*

+   +   +

De-Stressor Link

I am always amazed by how much damage stress does in our lives. I came across a very "pregnant" website, "giving birth" to many areas for recovery:

http://www.personal-recovery-tools.com/stress-management.html

Bushel or Bridge?

Living in-BE-tween

My life is "in between" right now, reminding me of the children's song "The Grand Old Duke of York," which we learned and acted out in elementary school. The chorus goes: "And when you're up, you're up, and when you're down you're down, but when you're only in between you're neither up nor down."

This, currently, is the story of my life: only in between and neither up nor down. I am in between job positions, having left a full-time job of twenty-five years after hitting bottom, going through treatment, and beginning again, reinventing myself. Should I do another internship, or some other job? Who knows what the #$*!?

Thank goodness I only have to live one day, one hour, one moment at a time. How appropriate that the word in the middle of "in between" is *be*. That's it! The word *be* is like *acceptance*, like *presence*, *patience*, and *being*. The *Big Book* states clearly, and many people in the program chant frequently, "Acceptance is the answer to all our problems for today."

Being is the answer to all our problems this day, at this moment. There is no time, so to speak, there is only now, only this moment. I do not have to worry about tomorrow or yesterday, only about living as much as possible in the present, not missing the mysteries that continue to unfold around me. *Why* is this so much more easily said than done? I guess that's the "recovery" part of recovery.

In light of this Light, I was talking to a doctor this morning in the hallway of the hospital. When I told her of my in-between situation, she said, "Are you afraid you might be flipping burgers?" I said, "No, I'm afraid I'll have to work more days at the 'madhouse,' as I call it, where I have worked for twenty months." On the one hand it's exactly where I need to be as I learn most about my character defects and how to grow through them. On the other hand It is a very stressful work environment, and though I've learned much about working with those in recovery, I had to begin at entry level pay as a resident assistant—in other words, 'gopher' and 'med-slave.' I'm not ungrateful—it can be a real blessing at times for me and others. It's just that it was a limited-time position to let me transition to full-time chaplain working with the same clientele. That did not work out for a number of reasons, including my inability or unwillingness to learn as much from the hard lined approach of the previous chaplain, as I did from the life-giving approach of my hospital supervisor. This frustration is accentuated by the greater fact of spending the past twenty-five years in a very fulfilling, well-paid senior pastor position. I am still struggling to adjust to such a momentous shift.

I said to the doctor, "I suppose if I were to work at flipping burgers, it would be 'hiding my light under a bushel?'" And she said right back, 'Or it could be a bridge over troubled waters." I liked that. It helps in the in-be-tween process. Such a clarifying truth also helps me in that it's not the quick clichés of "Oh, just trust God," or "One day at a time" or whatever. It's OK to just "be" when I'm in **be** tween.

"I believe, help my unbelief." Right where I'm at is OK. Regardless of these rare, blessed insights, the line from Jim Croce's song, "Operator" often surfaces in my brain: "I only wish my words could convince myself..."

Blessings together, In-BE-tween

Step 3

Made a decision to turn our will and our lives over to the care of God as we understood Him

Theme: Faith

The Program's Spiritual Steps 2,3,11

Transformation / Preparation

As we begin to turn our will and our lives over to the care of God as we understand God, a slow inner transformation takes place: our Higher Power begins to work in and through us, changing our thoughts and thereby our actions. A prayer emerged from within me recently when I was anticipating what was going to be a very difficult day, filled with possible emergency encounters, caring for patients as a chaplaincy intern. As my colleagues and I finished our morning meditation and joined hands for a circle prayer, the following came out of my mouth and heart: "God, go before us and prepare the way; help us get out of Your way; and help us not run away."

Our amazing, vigilant, powerful Higher Power promises to go before us to prepare the way, whatever we need to do or accomplish. He helps us get out of the way so He can work. And, when we see Him working through us, we will not wish to run away. He will continue to do for us, in us, and through us, what we cannot do for ourselves. What an awesome Higher-Powered-God!

+   +   +

Memorable Expressions from AA Meetings

AA meetings are like a study in the oral transmission of a recovery language. We listen and absorb, taking in what works and passing it on to others. Whether it is timeless wisdom or a gut-level reality experience, there is a beautiful freedom in meetings to speak the truth, our truth, whatever that may be. Here are a few from my recent meetings. I wrote them down and pass them to you…

> *"The 12 Steps keep me in line; the 12 Traditions keep the group in line."*

> *"I used to have the best friends money could buy!"*

> *"I had a real problem with God, but I realized that He brought me here. I wanted to die…my only reason to live were my two dogs."*

> *"I think I can call you my friends. I know I can lean on any one of you… but today is a happy day, and I don't need to."*

> *"I'm a periodic, episodic, problematic drunk."*

One woman named Barb stenciled above her bathroom mirror:

> *"You are looking at the problem!"*

*"The only thing that kept me alive was
my dog. I didn't know who was going
to take care of my dog if I was gone."*

Here are a couple of Eric's favorite phrases he
received from his father who is also in recovery:

*"Switching from liquor to weed is
like switching chairs on the Titanic."*

*"If you go with the same friends to
the same playground, you will end up
playing the same games."*

I quoted the late Father Martin, a well-known
Catholic priest who lectured on recovery:

*"Gratitude is the hinge on which the
door of recovery swings."*

Chiseling or Polishing?

I was blessed to be able to make a hospital visit both yesterday and today to a beautiful elderly woman who amidst her severe health problems was a shining example of someone who becomes stronger and more spiritual through her suffering. As I was speaking to her about all her health issues, she simply responded, "God has been so good to me. He's just polishing me right now."

That word polishing grabbed me. I began to think about my own life and recovery, with its pain, shame, healing, growing, and so much more that words cannot begin to describe. I thought that I rarely, if ever, use the word polishing when it comes to what I feel my Higher Power is doing in my life. Words like chiseling, drilling—as with a jackhammer, or even dynamiting away the destructive areas of my life, seem much more appropriate in describing my recovery process. But I like polishing. It reminds me of being a boy in Minneapolis and visiting Mr. Greystone at the end of our street, whose basement was filled with rock tumblers, always tumbling, constantly polishing rough-hewn rocks into something beautiful, revealing the stones' deep, rich colors.

Last night this polished woman had two heart attacks, but was brought back to life both times. When I visited her this morning, bringing her requested large-print devotional booklet, she was very tired but awake. She still had that peaceful glow about her that impressed me at first glance. When I said to her, "God was really polishing you last night," she smiled and said "He's so good to me, and has just a little more work to do."

I was amazed at her faith and openness. With all that polishing, it made me realize where her shine comes from. It also made me wonder if all God's polishing in this life is simply getting us ready to shine gloriously in the next!

"If I say, 'Surely the darkness shall fall on me,'
even the night shall be light about me;
Indeed, the darkness shall not hide from You,
but the night shines as the day; the darkness
and the light are both alike to You." (Ps.139:1)

Useful Stories Resurfacing

Sometimes useful stories that served as pieces of my recovery puzzle in years past later resurface to further illuminate just when I need them. Such is the case with the following story, "The Bike Ride," which helps me better understand my Higher Power as He continues to surface in my mind, heart, and soul.

The Bike Ride

Author Unknown

At first I saw God as my observer, my judge, keeping track of the things I did wrong, so as to know whether I merited Heaven or Hell when I die. He was out there, sort of like the President. I recognized His picture when I saw it, but I didn't really know Him.

But later on when I recognized my Higher Power, it seemed as though life was rather like a bike ride, but on a tandem bike, with God in the back helping me pedal. I don't know just when it was that He suggested we change places, but life has not been the same since...life with my Higher Power, that is. God makes life exciting.

When I had control, I knew the way. It was rather boring, but predictable. It was the shortest distance between two points. But when He took the lead, He knew delightful long cuts, up mountains, and through rocky places and at breakneck speeds. It was all I could do to hang on! Even though it looked like madness, He said, "Pedal!"

I worried and was anxious and asked, "Where are You taking me?" He laughed and didn't answer, and I started to trust. I forgot my boring life and entered into the adventure; and when I'd say, "I'm scared," He'd lean back and touch my hand.

He took me to people with gifts that I needed, gifts of healing, acceptance, and joy. They gave me their gifts to take on my journey; our journey, God's and mine.

And we were off again. He said, "Give the gifts away. They're extra baggage, too much weight." So I did, to the people we met, and I found that in giving I received, and still our burden was light.

I did not trust Him at first with control of my life. I thought he'd wreck it. But He knew bike secrets, knew how to make it bend to take sharp corners, jump to clear high places filled with rocks, fly to shorten scary passages.

I'm learning to shut up and pedal in the strangest places, and I'm beginning to enjoy the view and the cool breeze on my face with my delightful constant companion, my Higher Power.

And when I'm sure I can't do any more, He just smiles and says, "Pedal!"

Find Out What God Is Doing and Jump into the Middle of It!

This was one of those simple revelatory truths taught me by a wise church elder many years ago and it has always shaken me out of my lethargy. God, as I understand God, is always active, like fluent grace, ever wanting to flow more freely in and through my expanding wide-rivered-life, touching, healing, changing me and thereby others through me. Last night I was feeling spiritually weak—too many days of caring for others, "filling up their buckets" while mine was about empty. I was running on fumes, which can't even start my engine. I read for an hour in my reflection books, trying to find something to perhaps write a blog on—not for others at the time, but for myself. Something to crank my engine and rev this little car up to go somewhere---Nothing!

Then it hit me: it's been seven days without a meeting, and "Seven days without a meeting makes one weak!" I am thanking God this morning for Marty, my work supervisor, who gives me every Wednesday off for my four meetings: two AA, one with my sponsee between meetings, and one with my sponsor after the meetings. It fills me up. Thank you, God. This IS what God is doing, and I'm jumping into the middle of it.

HE must increase, I must decrease. I need to get out of the way and let Him work, like the legendary golfer Lee Trevino who has actually been struck twice by lightning while golfing. When asked what he learned after the first strike, he said "In case of a thunderstorm, stand in the middle of the fairway and hold up a one-iron. Not even God can hit a one-iron." When asked what he learned after the second strike, he said "When God wants to play through, you let Him."

God, please play through me this day, and help me continue to jump into the middle of what You are doing.

Acceptance

Since I do not studiously pour over the readings in the *Big Book,* I force myself to learn helpful snippets most weeks by bringing this recovery bible to my meetings, writing in the margins simple and often profound truths shared by others, and underlining quotes that have helped others stay sober and even saved their lives.

Last meeting a member said he went into a bar and saw a well-respected off-duty police officer sitting with a row of shots lined up in front of him. He would not even pick up the shots anymore because he didn't want people to see the trembling of his shaking hands, so he bent over and picked them up with his lips. The member was shocked to see the officer there, naively thinking that such professionals did not drink. He came up to him and said, "Excuse me, but if you drink all those shots, aren't you afraid you're going to die?" The officer, without hesitation, looked at him despairingly and said, "No! I'm afraid I'm going to live!"

The member never forgot these drunken, sobering words, sharing them freely over the years in his meetings. It gives a special insight into this disease when another attempts to kill himself because he is more afraid of living than dying! This same member read from the *Big Book of AA,* Fourth Edition, pp. 416–17:

At last, acceptance proved to be the key to my drinking problem. After I had been around AA for seven months, tapering off alcohol and pills, not finding the program working very well, I was finally able to say, "Okay, God. It is true that I—of all people, strange as it may seem, and even though I didn't give my permission—really, really am an alcoholic of sorts. And it's all right with me. Now what am I going to do about it?" When I stopped living in the problem and began living in the answer, the problem went away. From that moment on, I have not had a single compulsion to drink.

+   +   +

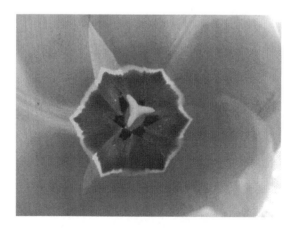

Freedom

I heard that great chorus from "Me and Bobby McGee" the other day: *"Freedom's just another word for nothing left to lose."* In many ways this relates to my alcoholism, my hitting bottom and thinking that after such major losses in my life, I had nothing left to lose. I could only begin to improve slowly, taking baby steps, getting on with a new life. With God's grace over the past two years and almost eight months, I am reinventing myself, one day at a time. It is such slow work, but I can actually see steady progress, one day at a time with limited expectations, or rather, realistic expectations. My Higher Power usually surprises me with much more than I have expected. This saying becomes truer every day: *My worst day sober is better than my best day drunk!*

Thank you God! And thanks to all in recovery, for keep'n on, keep'n on as we're all in this together!

Contentment

When is enough enough?

A rich industrialist from the North was horrified to find a Southern fisherman lying lazily beside his boat smoking a pipe. "Why aren't you out fishing?" asked the industrialist." "Because I have caught enough fish for today," said the fisherman. "Why don't you catch more than you need?" asked the industrialist. "What would I do with it?" asked the fisherman. "You could earn more money," was the reply. "With what you sell your extra fish for you could get a better motor and boat; you could go into deeper waters and catch more fish. You could buy nylon nets. You could catch more fish and make more money. Soon you could have two boats, then a fleet of boats, employees, and a real business. Then you would be rich like me." The fisherman asked, "Then what would I do?" The industrialist said, "Then you could sit down and enjoy life." The fisherman said, "What do you think I'm doing now?!"

What do I really need to be content? More friends? Another relationship? A better paying job? One of our local university professors starts his Psych 101 class by asking his students "Why are you here? Why are you going to college?" He gets a range of answers, from getting a good job to being successful to living the American dream. He continues asking them again and again, writing all their answers on one side of the board.

Finally one class member answers, "I just want to be happy!" The professor writes the word *HAPPINESS* on the other side of the board and circles it. He then asks his students "Does achieving all the things on this side of the board equal happiness?" Yes? No? If not, what does? This professor then goes on to discreetly share his spirituality as the source of personal happiness in his life. What simple, practical insights deduced from the minds, and hearts of his students!

Happiness, contentment, serenity—gracious gifts from our Higher Power given as we walk our talk in recovery—are more precious and powerful than any degree, success, silver, or gold.

Unconditional Love

Unconditional love is not so much about how we receive and endure each other, as it is about the deep vow to never, under any condition, stop bringing the flawed truth of who we are to each other. --Mark Nepo

I love this quote. It gets at the heart of recovery and the deep, recovering heart. I have often thought too much about the difference between unconditional love and tough love. Who knows and who cares, as they both collide in "the wisdom to know the difference." As we live out our faith and recovery we will continue to discover how to bring out that flawed truth when we stop hiding our character defects, being afraid of what others may think or say about us, or do to us. Are we *willing to take risks?* This is a daily qualification in going beyond my denial and living in the land of growth and healing; my goal for this day, for each day.

We can be the moon reflecting the sun's light. We can be the daily miracle which reflects the spiritual Light towards ourselves and those around us. Conversely, we can also touch others with darkness and things negative. We are always reflective witnesses, able to shine forth light as well as darkness for good and for evil. This was a resonating truth for me from today's reading. It spoke of uncovering the healing openness in me because of how open others have been with me. I cannot help but think of this transforming openness in our AA meetings and 12-step recovery program, as well as my weekly growth meetings with my sponsor and my sponsees.

I mentioned to my sponsor what I thought was a universal truth, certainly one in my life, but he sort of turned it on its head. I stated how few really good friends we have in our lives; we are able to count them on one hand. He said that for him it's just the opposite: because he has always been so open to almost everyone in his life, people have been attracted to him and he has gained a whole network of friends that he can go to whenever he needs to, even as they come to him.

Leave it to my amazing, crazy sponsor to challenge a truth in my life that may have been more of an excuse to isolate, being afraid to get too close to others for fear of being hurt. He truly has an open-door policy; on any given day I may stop by. We are usually not alone.

Higher Power, how amazing that bringing out my flawed truth frees others to do the same. Thank you for giving me the strength and desire to do so.

The Mountain of Unconditional Love

So many people ask that eternal (or is it 'infernal') question: "Why am I here?"

Through my ongoing relationships and daily recovery reflections, it is abundantly clear that if we are here for any reason it is *to receive and share unconditional love.* This truth ties in strongly with our recovery and healing. We are empowered to tap into the unconditional love source of our Higher Power, whatever or whoever that might be. When we do, we receive love that loves us in spite of ourselves, even when we cannot love ourselves nor feel any love from those around us. I am empowered and changed by the love of my Higher Power. It forces me to love myself, and, as I do, I can love others unconditionally—even those who have hurt me. *I can love them the way I am being loved.*

What circumstances in our lives are conducive for a Higher Power to use to get through to our hearts? Anything and everything: job, loneliness, children, family, future, past, and so on. This mountain of love in my life is impossible to get away from. I can't go around. I am forced to embrace it, to climb it, and as I do, the panorama is something I've never seen before! I want to stay there, but I cannot—I need to let others know, especially the masses in the deepest, darkest valleys that have no clue such a mountain even exists, let alone the truth that they too can receive the power to climb to its summit.

~ The greatest thing in all the world
is to love and be loved ~

Divine Collisions

One of the blessings of working in our local hospital is the opportunity to see the creative works of artists every couple of months. These displays are inspirational and encourage the daily visitors who flow through the halls, often deeply stressed by their loved one's hospitalization. Today a new artist was setting up her display. I have not personally met any of the artists; I usually admire their artistry from a distance, feeling somewhat detached from the work itself. Earlier today I chided myself for not looking more closely at the display just taken down—beautiful underwater photographs of a variety of luminescent salt-water creatures. I procrastinated and they are gone. I did not form a connection with their creator.

As the artist was hanging her creations this afternoon, I stopped briefly, sharing with her that I liked the style of her work—its variety, diversity, and texture. She shared with me the background and inspiration of a few of her pieces. That was it;

she was busy working to get her exhibit finalized.

As I walked the quiet halls later this evening, I felt more of a connection to the display. I don't know the artist and only visited with her briefly, yet there is a connection to her work that inspires me in a stronger way than if I did not have the encounter.

The parallel here with my Higher Power is obvious: I have a connection. I used to be detached, passing through life, living for myself, thinking I was in control. I thought I was the creator and master of my own destiny. That attitude reached its worst potential in extreme drinking and slow self-destruction. But I met the Artist again. It would be more accurate to say "the Artist met me"—in a violent collision that literally knocked me out, but at the same time woke me up. I had a deep, passionate encounter with the lover of my soul. It was extremely painful, and I continue to dig out from under that divine tryst—but what an affair! Oh, what a night in hindsight, in Divine Sight!

And now, when I am not running away, I am beginning to experience the love of my Lover, often in the form of others' love toward me. I am learning to better love myself—why is this such a life's work? Perhaps because I've spent a lifetime not accepting it or realizing it for a myriad of reasons that were certainly fueled by alcohol.

Today I am thankful for "divine collisions" that happen between my Higher Power and myself, but genuinely lived out in my collisions with others.

Confused But Not Lost

"The race is not to the swift, but to those who keep on running!"

In the midst of everything going on in my life and love, it's good to remember that though I may be confused at times—deeply confused, even troubled—I am never lost. I know I'm on the right road. I know where this road leads, and I know that I am not only surrounded by others on this journey, but I am being pushed forward, sometimes carried, sometimes carrying others.

In an iTunes celebrity podcast hosted by Keith Urban and featuring great performers and the music that has most inspired them, Urban shared lyrics from U2's song "One." The part of the song that he said most inspired him was the phrase *We get to carry each other.* Urban said, "It's not preachy like 'You got to carry your brother!'" He is saying we have each been given the privilege of carrying another, even as we ourselves have been carried. That phrase perfectly summarizes the best of both recovery and spirituality for me.

I was reminded of this truth when running my first marathon over twenty years ago. As I reached mile fifteen, I saw a guy slowing down and giving up. I slowed down, then stopped and said gently, "You can do it! We've gone through too many months of training to give up now without finishing!" His response was simply, "There's always someone like you in these races," and he slowly began to run.

About five miles later, after hitting the wall at mile twenty, my natural reserves were depleted. I was cramping up every few blocks, stopping, and trying to stretch to be able to keep going. Just when I thought I wouldn't make it, the same guy I had encouraged earlier came by and said, "You can do it! We've gone through so many months of training to give up now without finishing!" I couldn't believe it! It was definitely a strong sign for me, and provided just enough extra gas to start my engines, helping me believe that maybe I could make it to the finish line.

I finished the race, running through painful cramps, but never saw that runner again. Maybe he was an "angel unawares." He certainly was for me.

I thank my Higher Power for the angels in my daily life who minister through answered prayers and words of encouragement, as well as through deep, emotional pain and crises. I do believe all things are working together for the good—for our eternal good.

Peace and light as we run the race together, having gone through so many "months of training," we can't give up now without finishing!

A woman once went on a journey to
a distant city. She was unfamiliar with the route,
became confused, and took the wrong road.
She stopped her car and asked a passing stranger,
"Can you help me? I am lost."

"Where are you headed?" asked the stranger.
"I'm going to Boston," the traveler answered.
"Then you are not lost.
You know where you are going.
You just need directions."

Summer

A perfect summer day is when the sun is shining, the breeze is blowing, the birds are singing, and the lawn mower is broken.

—James Dent

Steps 4-7: Clean Up

The healing sunshine of summer reveals to us that not only are we survivors, but we are moving beyond surviving to thriving. The sunshine of God's grace can overwhelm us and strengthen us, gifting us with an empowered new life!

Step 4

Made a searching and fearless moral inventory of ourselves.

Theme: Courage

In these Steps I seek the truth about my strengths and my weaknesses. I admit those truths to God, to myself, and to another human being and then I become entirely ready for God to remove my shortcomings

Brutal Honesty

Brutal honesty—a fearful phrase for me after hiding and isolating myself for so many years, barely keeping my head above water during the last few years of my increased drinking before having a near-death experience and hitting bottom.

Though extremely difficult, brutal honesty was part of my inpatient treatment. It helped me slowly apply this healing action to my recovery because I saw others modeling it for me in their sharing. I was blown away! It was so powerful to hear the naked truth from others, to hear them giving it up, letting it go, going to the depths of their pain and sharing to the best of their ability in a safe environment with other people who were just as torn and broken. This life-changing honesty empowers me to practice and strive for the same; it is what surfaces every week at every meeting I attend. I see more clearly the truth that sets one free manifesting itself in surprising ways.

This past week's AA meeting topic was "Where You Were and Where You Are Now." The honesty flowed from so many, culminating in stories of suicide and other near-death experiences, each encouraging the others to be more honest and brutally open.

One member shared with the group a memory of going to jail and asking the officer why he had taken away his belt and shoelaces, "To keep you from hanging yourself!" the officer replied. Another member, with less than four months of sobriety, talked of taking a couple of bottles' worth of pills and then taking a knife to herself, not knowing what she had done until two days later when she awakened in the hospital. Brutal honesty surfaced around the table and most of us who shared gave thanks to our Higher Power that we have been given many second chances to live freely without drugs and alcohol, without those substances that so readily assisted us in our self-destruction.

Such honest sharing reminded me of a one of our regular AA members who frequently blurts out, "I was afraid of living! I was more afraid of living than I was of dying!" This same member, now with over two years of sobriety, has done a complete one-eighty and is one of the most positive and upbeat persons I know. Her joy is contagious and she almost always makes me laugh, richly blessing my day!

Thank you, Higher Power, because I no longer need to be afraid of living. Nothing is so bad that I have to self-destruct because of the pain. Nothing is so bad that You cannot carry me through any of it with daily healing. Thank you for giving me brutal honesty—as much as I am able to share at this time. Please continue to help me share more and receive more of the same from others.

"Roll...Out...Those...Lazy, Hazy, Crazy Days of Summer"

Comfortably Living on the Edge

Despite the daily difficulties that life throws at us, one of the more helpful recovery phrases I am growing into is being "comfortable in my own skin." A contrary phrase might be: "When I am not comfortable being who I am, I use, misuse and abuse myself and others in my life." When I get to know my strengths and weaknesses—how they are revealed in healthy ways—I am able to live more comfortable in my own skin.

Healthy recovery is knowing we are better equipped every day to live in the midst of whatever happens. Although daily living for all people *is* chaos, we are given the tools to manage such chaos. In light of this, I realize that I am most comfortable or most alive when I am living on the edge, where most change happens. In a negative light, perhaps such "edginess" is being an adrenaline junkie. That name characterizes all of us who abuse substances and alter our moods in unhealthy escapes. But there is a positive side to frequently finding ourselves on the edge of life—it helps us see how we are hardwired by our Creator.

Some of this hard-wiring includes our personality types (in my case, ENFP on the Myers-Briggs scale), my birth order, life history, personal trauma, and gifts of expression through being an artist, musician, writer, and much more. I find myself loitering at the crossroads of daily living. Though the edges of these crossroads have slowly and often painfully changed over the years in more healthy ways, I still find myself on that precipice where life can change in an instant, for better or for worse.

A personal example of this was needing to push my body to the edge in my mid-thirties by not only running two marathons but also by setting a seven-minute-mile pace to achieve my three-hour goal and place in the top ten percent of the thousands of runners. I have loved being in the emergency room while on call as a chaplaincy intern, caught up in deep family crises, as well as experiencing all the gut-wrenching emotions swirling around death and funerals.

There is that special energy not only in the presence of new life being born, but also with the birth of changes to the mind and heart from teaching and preaching. There is that survival-instinct thrill from battling the elements and dressing in multiple layers to survive a windy, snowy, twenty-below-zero day. Is this why so many in recovery still live in Minnesota?

There is also the edge of explosive anger of self and others, yet there is also tremendous personal growth when that anger is managed and resolved. And though the death of others can cause deep pain and sorrow, those in healthy recovery learn about acceptance of all situations, believing that their Higher Power will continue to work through *all* things in their lives for good.

For those of us in recovery, managing life on the edge can help us live out our destinies and purposes in a greater way, perhaps the only way. I believe that daily events on the edge force us to step out of our comfort zones and embrace our fears, wrestling them until they provoke personal transformation.

In some ways our whole lives are lived on the edge, the edge of new developments. Whether we perceive them as good or bad, they just *are*. It's the five percent of what happens to us and the ninety-five percent of how we respond. By the grace and power given us, will we become bitter, falling off the edge, or better, living more comfortably on the edge in our own skin?

Inner Peace

(This is so true!)

✓ If you can start the day without caffeine...

✓ If you can always be cheerful, ignoring aches and pains...

✓ If you can resist complaining and boring people with your troubles...

✓ If you can eat the same food every day and be grateful for it...

✓ If you can understand when your loved ones are too busy to give you any time...

- ✓ If you can take criticism and blame without resentment...

- ✓ If you can conquer tension without medical help...

- ✓ If you can sleep without the aid of drugs...

Then You Are Probably...

The Family Dog!

~ Good old Nikki - our family dog ~

Treasures of Darkness

I came across a phrase this morning from my readings that caught my attention: *Treasures of Darkness.* It was used in referring to the unforeseen blessings that can only be born from our darkest days. I like that. This certainly is a theme of the recovery life. Just about everyone I have met in healthy recovery are going and growing through their pain towards healing. What does this mean? The popular spiritual phrase used in the 60s comes to mind: *self-actualization.* The dictionary definition of that phrase is:

The achievement of one's full potential through creativity, independence, spontaneity, and a grasp of the real world.

I am using it to refer to the idea of becoming all we can be—living more of our destiny and not floundering in our "density." We can be daily empowered to take the recovering high road, not the getting-high road with "Slick, the Slickster"—that self-destructive side of us that would just as soon destroy us yesterday than allow us another grateful breath.

I was part of a gut-wrenching Grief/Loss group the other night, but a helpful recovery phrase surfaced when someone said, "I guess we really just have to move toward the pain to heal, not run away from it." It's like the spiritual song "Swing Low Sweet Chariot": *"So high you can't get over it, so low, you can't get under it, so wide, you can't go around it so you have to go through the door!"* And we don't have to wonder if behind the door is the lady or the tiger. The nice thing about living out an actualized 12-step program is when we go through the "Doors of Recovery" which grace-fully swing open for us, it doesn't matter what's on the other side; we can use it all for our continued recovery…Come what may!

IT'S ALLLLLLLL GOOD! IT'S ALL GRRRRRRRREAT!

Anger As Hidden Fear

I was reminded at a meeting this week about the deep connection between anger and fear. We began our meeting, as always, asking if anyone needed any special time to process something heavy on their hearts affecting their sobriety. A regular member with almost three years' sobriety shared that she was very close to relapsing last night because she was physically threatened by another and felt so much anger, because she felt so much fear.

She managed not to drink by "hanging" on the phone with friends for hours, calling the police, and getting the offender locked up. From there her fears multiplied in anticipation that her perpetrator would take revenge on her upon his release. Despite this paralysis, she felt deep relief after sharing and receiving the group's support, prayers and caring.

As the meeting progressed with all freely sharing, most confirmed the connection between anger and fear in their own recovery, learning that strong recovery is not the absence of fear, but controlling the fear—even using its energy for constructive purposes.

It was a cathartic process for me, remembering the times I have experienced intense anger lying behind intense fear. The end results demonstrated the power of the group, with the whole becoming much greater than the sum of its parts.

I pray for a deeper understanding of my anger that is an outgrowth of my deepest fears, before it turns inward and manifests itself in depression.

Some All-Too-Human Prayers

❖ Lord, help me to relax about insignificant details beginning tomorrow at 7:41:23 a.m. EST.

❖ God, help me to consider people's feelings, even if most of them *are* hypersensitive.

❖ God, help me to take responsibility for my own actions, even though they're usually *not* my fault.

❖ God, help me to not try to *run* everything. But, if You need some help, please feel free to ask me!

❖ Lord, help me to be more laid back and help me to do it *exactly* right.

❖ God, help me to take things more seriously, especially laughter, parties, and dancing.

❖ God, give me patience, and I mean right now!

❖ Lord, help me not be a perfectionist. (Did I spell that correctly?)

❖ God, help me to finish everything I sta...

❖ God, help me to keep my mind on one th—Look, a bird!—ing at a time.

❖ God, help me to do only what I can, and to trust you for the rest. And would you mind putting that in writing?

❖ Lord, keep me open to others' ideas, wrong though they may be.

❖ Lord, help me be less independent, but let me do it my way.

❖ Lord, help me follow established procedures today. On second thought, I'll settle for a few minutes.

❖ Lord, help me slow down and not rushthroughwhatIdo. + Amen.

Believing Is Seeing

The Wright Brothers' almost childish faith that they could build a machine which would fly was the mainspring of their accomplishment. Without that, nothing could have happened. We agnostics and atheists were sticking to the idea that self-sufficiency would solve our problems. When others showed us that God-sufficiency worked with them, we began to feel like those who had insisted the Wrights would never fly. We were seeing another kind of flight, a spiritual liberation from this world, people who rose above their problems.

Alcoholics Anonymous, pp. 52-53

I love this short, powerful reading from Bill W. It reminds me of one of my favorite mantras: "Growing up to be a Child." We grow up by growing in child-like faith not "childish-faith"—big difference. I think of how childish and immature I was in many ways in my days of use, misuse and abuse. Most things centered on me and on what I wanted. I pressed my gifts too far and they became my defects—from loving people and using things to using people and loving things. What a breakthrough it was for me to begin to know a Higher Power that had freed me to soar in healthy, recovering ways.

My transformation from a god of my own understanding—that would be me—to a God that freed me to fly has been a liberation lasting decades; a process that has given me the glue that holds my life and perhaps all life together.

I remember my spiritual progression. I got involved in Eastern meditation and Christianity after high school, realizing there really was a God who loved me unconditionally! Whatever that meant, I knew it was life-changing. I then realized not only did this God love me, but He also graced me with the gifts I needed to fulfill the life-calling He had hardwired into me.

As I have eased on down the recovery road, my Higher Power has brought me to another freeing understanding that I frequently share with others: He chooses to use the worst things in my life—my deepest shame—to demonstrate not only how much He loves and forgives me, but how He miraculously recycles everything! Nothing is wasted. I am able to help others the way I've been helped; I can understand in ways that I have been understood, continuing to better understand myself in effective recovery.

There is a glorious freedom in daily recovery

to fly above my struggles and problems, not ignoring them or stuffing them out of sight, but taking the grace freely given to mount up on wings of eagles. Though I may still be grounded on some days, on the ground or in the air who cares, as long as I am clean and sober? I'd rather be grounded sober than flying "high"!

I'm thankful that we can fly the friendly skies of recovery together.

Step 5

Admitted to God, to ourselves, and to another human being the exact nature of our wrongs.

Theme: Integrity

Steps 4 and 5 are about owning up.

The Heart of the Fifth Step

Remembering the Big Picture

There are many reasons we do the Fourth and Fifth Steps in recovery, but the heart of this process is the heart of all recovery: to stop destroying ourselves through alcohol and drugs and live a productive life, one we were meant to live. We learn very quickly about the 12 Steps, but it usually takes many meetings to start learning about the complementary 12 Traditions. Many meetings alternate each month, using a Step one week and a Tradition the following week.

I am slowly learning the wisdom of both as presented in the very helpful condensed book we call "The 12 X 12", or *The 12 Steps and the 12 Traditions*. Many people in recovery have purchased a leather case that houses the *Big Book* and this little gem. And, to summarize, you will often hear, "The 12 Steps keep the alcoholic in line, while the 12 Traditions keep the group in line." The most important requirement for anyone around the world to be a member of Alcoholics Anonymous is what Tradition 3 states in a simple, powerful, and unmistakable way:

The only requirement for AA membership is a desire to stop drinking.

I need to remember this constantly, not only to keep in mind that I am a full-fledged member of AA, but also to never forget that anyone and everyone is welcome at any meeting I attend, if they simply have a desire to stop drinking. So, I write it this way to help me never forget:

THEONLYREQUIREMENT........THE
ONLYREQUIREMENT.................
THEONLYREQUIREMENT........THE
ONLYREQUIREMENT........THEONL
YREQUIREMENT........THEONLYRE
QUIREMENT........THEONLYREQUIR
EMENT........THEONLYREQUIREME
NT........THEONLYREQUIREMENT...
.....THEONLYREQUIREMENT........T
HEONLYREQUIREMENT........THEO
NLYREQUIREMENT........THEONLY
REQUIREMENT........THEONLYREQ
UIREMENT........THEONLYREQUIRE
MENT.......THEONLYREQUIREMENT
IS A DESIRE TO STOP DRINKING!

Our Last Day on Earth

What if I knew this was my last day on earth? Our retired neighbors lost the largest and most beautiful of all their trees in their front yard last week due to heavy rain and eighty-to-one hundred-mph straight winds. In the midst of his cleanup I yelled across the street, "Are you going to plant another tree?" He called out in quiet futility, "What good would that do? I won't be here to enjoy it." I couldn't help but walk slowly toward him and say, "Martin Luther was asked what he would do if he knew this was his last day on earth. He responded by saying, 'I'd go out and plant a tree.'" My neighbor just shook his head and kept splitting wood from the fallen tree he had personally planted over forty years ago when he built his house.

I have used this end-of-our-world question in teaching spiritual truths to students over the years: "What would you do today if this was your last day on earth?" Many of them say things like: "I would tell people how much I love them"; "I'd pray a lot"; "I'd forgive anyone I could think of." One woman said, "I'd write down all the things I do, because after I'm gone my husband would not have a clue." My obvious response after all the sharing was, "Well, you don't know if this is our last day or not, so why wouldn't you attempt to do all things you just shared?" Is it because we don't want to deal with this very real reality? I believe the phrase: 'Until we begin to deal with our own deaths, we cannot begin to truly live.'"

On January 24, 1988, my father-in-law was teaching his wife's Sunday-school class in northern Minnesota. He asked the young students, "If you were to die today, do you think you would go to heaven?" He went on to share how he felt strongly that he would, because of his faith in God and in God's promises to him. That afternoon, in the middle of a winter storm, my father-in-law went out to check the roads for his family who had called him as they drove home from Wisconsin. A snowplow ran into him and he died in seven minutes from internal bleeding.

This past winter, as I shoveled the sometimes beautiful and often brutal snow from my driveway, this question had a way of surfacing. If I knew this was my last day to live, would I be shoveling this snow? Probably not, but it was a good thought—I'd like to be advanced enough in life to have the calm and peace of being present, enjoying shoveling snow for the last time on Earth. Perhaps some of you are thinking, "What a blessing to shovel snow for the last time!" But I think I'd know where I'd be—with all my siblings, family and loved ones, talking, praying, laughing, hugging, maybe even eating those better-than-sex homemade bars and cakes that are as decadent as they are addictive, not worrying about calories, extra pounds, or bad cholesterol.

About fifteen years ago, our neighbor Dave was diagnosed with cancer and was told he had only a year to live. It was tragic. He was only forty years old, had a loving wife named Karla, was athletic and strong and worked as the physical education teacher at a local junior high school. But Dave was amazing and his faith and zest for life were even more so. While he was still coherent and his spirits high, he invited a number of us in the neighborhood to his home just to say goodbye—to talk about life and things he loved and how he appreciated us all. We bought three six-foot evergreen trees and planted them in Dave and Karla's back yard.

Dave died that spring, but I often think of him as I walk the golf course and look over at the three evergreen trees we planted, now standing over twenty feet high. How good it was to tell him how much we loved him before he died, when he could fully receive it. Why does it sometimes take a funeral to get us to share our heartfelt words?

I know that for many people, the depths of recovery have been a death and a resurrection—living their days like their last! *I pray for myself that my Higher Power can help me do a better job of that.*

Getting Rid of the Skunks

We had a bad problem with skunks last month—our lawn barely survived. In twenty-three years at the same house and same yard, we have never had this problem before. I'm not a pest-control expert, but something tells me the reason we had these tenacious varmints this year is because part of our lawn is the worst it's been in twenty-three years. The city put in water and sewer a decade ago, tearing up the street and half our front yard. They replaced our beautiful grass with cheap crabgrass stuff that has multiplied tenfold, despite our use of an every-other-year Chem-Lawn kind of service.

They only come out at night. Not just one skunk now, but a family of skunks. And why do they come? To dig grubs out of our yard. And where do they dig for them??? Yes, under the worst, faded, slightly brown grass. And whose yard on the block—one of the few without a sprinkler system—has the worst grass? Yes, ours. So, which is probably the only yard on the block where almost every morning reveals another new dirt pile from the skunk family? Right again! Damn those skunks! But it's not their fault. They are just doing what they do to survive and thrive—and they sure are thriving at our expense!

So what do you do? We've left big flood lights on all night—our neighbors liked that! Our neighbors down the trail had the same problem and pumped loud music through outdoor speakers at all hours of the night—it sounded and looked like a prisoner-of-war camp. I've gone out at all hours of the night with a BB gun; my wife wants me to borrow a .22 pistol from my sponsor, but that would be messy, not to mention very smelly and very illegal in our neighborhood—as in felony. I've had enough consequences over the past couple of years to last me a lifetime.

So what do we do? The pest control company seemed cost-prohibitive because they had to come out twice to get the job done. But, not to worry. Our lawn-care company said they would come out and put on a grubicide spray which would kill the grubs, eliminating the reason the skunks came in the first place. That was two weeks ago and we haven't seen any since.

My recovery application: The poor crab grass that multiplies over the years and brings the varmints that destroy my life are my poor habits, lack of meetings, relapse, and my life in general going to seed: a perfect invitation to invasive pests. The solution? The 12 Steps and the life-giving 12 promises, which bring the richest, thickest, and most beautifully groomed lawn/life on the block! After twenty-three years, my neighbors will be amazed (before we are half through), and the value of their homes (and lives) might even increase!

Living With and Through
The Shame and Pain

Living with and through the shame, how does *that* happen? How is that really possible? I can only speak of how it is happening in my life.

My goal: Continue to get in touch with unaddressed pain and shame issues from my past, allowing God, myself, and other human beings to assist in my healing and restoration to the person my Higher Power created me to be. Some have asked, "Why do you want to get in touch with shame in your life?" My response would be that I do it for the same reason we move toward pain in our grief and loss in order to heal. It's not dragging up or dredging the dysfunctional depths to find all the shame I can, it's about dealing with the shame that still lies buried away from fear and exposure to reality's bright light. It's not something I can do daily, but I strive for that in a variety of ways. My Higher Power keeps kicking me in that direction, even though it leaves some loving bruises on my tender ego and easily bruised flesh.

This goal is impossible for me to do because I have no power—I am powerless over my disease and my addiction. Left to myself, I *will* self-destruct, resulting in jail, institutions, death, or at best, injury to many other people till I die prematurely. But there is One who has all power, and I am thankful I have found that One—or have been graciously found.

People like to quote that God "works through all things for the good to those who love Him" (Romans 8:28), and I do believe that amazing promise, but I could fill pages with other verses and stories of people who hated God, who killed and tortured others who believed in Him, who were minutes away from death, swearing at God and mocking Him, yet who came to know the truth that set them free! Amazing grace, how sweet the sound.

What causes such personal transformation? Is it because we pray hard enough? Is it because we are such good people? Is it because we can speak in tongues and go to church or synagogue every Sunday or Sabbath? No! Hell, no! It is because God has all power and is gracious and loving beyond all human understanding. He causes rain to fall on the just and unjust. He loved the world so much that He gave, and said about hell, *NO!!!*

It's not about us. ***It's not about us!*** We are dead. We have no power. It's God, however we understand God, who makes us alive. It's this Power that restores us, empowers us, and turns our mourning into dancing, and our painful shame into healing, giving us beauty for ashes. This is the gracious One. Left to ourselves we will die, but in His hands, we will live *forever!*

This is beginning to sound like a sermon, and "people would rather see a sermon than read one any day." But if you have read this far, I pray it has been a gracious, liberating, freeing sermon. I no longer need to hang my head in shame, though it has taken me years of sobriety and serenity to get to this point. I no longer keep my eyes down when I go to the mall or grocery store or theater, wondering who will see me and if they do, what they will ask me and how I will answer? Now I go out wondering whom I will see—who my Higher Power will put in my path. God knows my shameful past and is able to see that my scars are still there, but they are becoming beautiful. Again, this doesn't happy every day, but it's happening more all the time, like the saying "I'm not all that I want to be, but I'm not what I used to be."

This is all so amazing! It reminds me of a life-changing book I read years ago called *Hind's Feet On High Places,* by Hannah Hurnard. It's an allegory about the life of "Much Afraid," who lives in the dark valley with her "Fearing" relatives. She is depressed and has no power until she meets the Good Shepherd on High Places, or initially in the deep valleys, just when she can go no further. In fact, the only way she is transformed is by taking the hands of her two closest companions, "Sorrow" and "Suffering," as they lift her to the highest places of joy and peace. Her Loving Shepherd then gives her a new name—and a new being—one of "Grace and Glory."

May our Higher Power continue to give us the grace to be transformed from Much-Afraid to Grace and Glory.

Breaking Family Cycles Though Our Fifth Step

Part of my Fourth and Fifth Step processes involved letting go of past actions that haunted and controlled me. Through that ego-deflating process I was given the inner strength I needed in order to be as brutally honest as possible. Many of my demons were exorcized by the sobering light of recovery and they headed for the door! They still try to return through a partially cracked back door I still carelessly leave open, but living out the Steps assists in keeping the shadows at bay. The Fifth Step confessional process helped me in remembering how I got through my dad's alcohol abuse growing up, as well as his sudden, premature death over twenty years ago as his disease caught up with him.

I know I got through it by the grace of God, but that grace was slow, painful, and took many detours through the valley of the shadow. Many recovery issues surfaced for me and my other four siblings, not the least of which was my sister's courageous willingness—and need—to share with us the sexual abuse she endured from my father while growing up. Her sharing was bold and necessary, shattering family skeletons in the closet. Though such revelations were terribly painful for my mother and all of us to hear, they were essential to allow real healing to begin.

I did not know how much control my father had over me—and how much I had had over my father—until I finally decided, through anger and some healthy adult-children-of-alcoholics teaching, to call him, yell at him, and tell him "It's over!" I told him in clear, concise terms, "I'm no longer calling you during the holidays or any days, because I never know if you're going to be drunk and most of the times you are, *whether you're a fucking functional drunk or not!*"

I was amazed by the voicemail my father left me the next day at my office after he sobered up. He was crying, saying "we can work this thing out." I felt I had taken away his power and control over me; the tables had been turned, and I received the needed strength to get on with living. Though it may not sound like it, my actions created healthy boundaries for me; it was my only way out, trapped in an enmeshed, deeply codependent family system.

It's imperative that we pray, plan, and find ways to break free that work for our systems. We will receive the needed strength to break destructive life cycles holding us hostage by honestly working the Steps. Although it is a slow, often painful process, it is deeply rewarding and life-changing.

After my dad's death I thought I'd be relieved. He was gone, out of my life, I was free of that controlling obligation and pain and so much more. But I was miserable. I cried intermittently for days. Daily journaling gave me no answers: "Why am I so sad when I thought I'd feel so relieved?" I kept writing and questioning, seeking some kind of understanding. Finally it surfaced, and it has been a breakthrough in understanding grief and healing both for myself and others ever since.

I realized, now that my father was dead-- really gone, *I never would have the relationship I'd always thought I would have, or that I'd hoped for.* Now it would *never* happen. Even though it never could have happened given the way things developed, I had always hoped against hope. I learned that I had to begin grieving for the confused seven-year-old boy who stood on the living room steps, listening to my mother telling me that my father had left and would not be coming back. "Was it my fault?" "Could I have done something different to keep him from leaving?" I began grieving that loss and slowly began my letting-go journey.

I still have not been to my father's grave, but perhaps my older brother and I will go one of these years; that would be healing in our relationship with our father as well as with each other.

There is a phrase that helps me understand this difficult healing process: "Life needs to be lived forward, but it can only be understood backwards." One of the most important things I learned about lessening the ultimate grief we may experience when a significant figure in our life dies is to do whatever I can do to let go before their departure. Any contact I can have—even tense contact with some kind of boundaries—the further along I'll be when they are gone.

Whatever it takes. Whatever that means for your situation. Even if that meant for me to get up enough strength to yell on the phone and say "I'm *not* going to take this shit anymore." Such bold, empowered efforts help in reclaiming who we are—our strength, our identities, our voices. This not only breaks the cycle for us, but also for future generations.

Dear Healing God of my understanding.
You know me so much better than I know myself.
Help me let go of the crippling pain and shame
in my life more each day. Help me know that you
are using everything in my life. Please continue to
carry me through the hard times, and, in turn, give
me the grace and desire to assist you—being
Your Hands—in carrying others.

Step 6

Were entirely ready to have God remove all these defects of character

Theme: Willingness

The Garbage in Our Homes

Part-1

We all have garbage in our homes. Every day it grows and increases, and if nothing is done about it, the whole house not only begins to stink, but will eventually produce the unhealthy byproducts of bugs, rodents, and disease. Why would we ever want things like that to grow in our homes or in our lives?

Our defects of character are like garbage in our lives that need to be dealt with. With our recovery comes the strength and desire our Higher Power gives us; we become willing and ready to have God remove these stinking, self-destructive defects. It's like preparing for surgery, as we cannot operate on ourselves. We need God's professional skill that can assist us in our healing. We become ready and willing to place ourselves in position for garbage-removal surgery.

Therefore, if we are empowered and motivated, we take the garbage out every couple of days to the cans or dumpster in our garage or on the side of our homes, where it waits for garbage pickup day. This necessary discipline is much easier to do in our homes and in our minds than in our daily actions. But that is what active sobriety is all about. Thank God we have a God that not only loves to help us sort through *all* our garbage, but loves to pick up that garbage. Our Higher Power's all-time favorite thing to do is to *recycle all our garbage* and make it useful again. "Are you kidding me? Useful again? *Garbage?!*" How can the very stuff that needs to be thrown out of our lives become useful again? Because that's the secret of a healthy, healing life—The Secret Recycler, our Higher Power! Amazing and true!

(Part 2 of this healing process comes in Step 7, p 143)

The Terrible Illusion of Urgency

*What we need is always harshly and beautifully right
before us, disguised in the wrapping of our nearest
urgency.*—Mark Nepo, *The Book of Awakening,* February 24

The phrase "tyranny of the urgent" comes to
mind as I read one of my morning reflections. Like
the above quote, it is as amazing as it is simple. I
may cry out, praying over and over again, "Higher
Power, show me the way! Help me! I am so
overwhelmed! I don't think I can make it!" At the
risk of trying to speak for my Higher Power, let me
simply paraphrase His possible response:

*"Ken, why so anxious, what's so urgent? Look
a little closer: in these urgent needs that you paint
as so extreme lies the answer. You know the truth,
but you just don't want to deal with it. I will give
you the desire to desire it, and the power to
overpower it. You are powerless, but I will give you
the power to let go and let Me!"*

I have found a pathetic scenario, common in
church-work vocations, full-time ministry, and the
everyday Christianity of the masses. If God hears it
once each day, He must hear it a billion times, even
after He's provided the answer. People cry and cry
and cry, "God, show me the way!" when the Way is
right in front of them. God's true will is as clear as
the nose on their faces, but they don't want to
accept it or do it. It's like the spiritual phrase says:
"Anyone can die for God, but try living for Him!"

This is obvious and easy to write, but difficult to regularly pray, let go, and believe. How good for me and for all of us in recovery to receive those grace-filled glimpses of light and truth each day that let us know that the God of our understanding is doing for us what we cannot do for ourselves.

I am being carried amidst paralyzing fears and tears. A recovery friend shared with me recently her gift from her Higher Power of pure joy. That gift was brought out through her inner physical healing and her getting out into God's creation. That touched and empowered me, not allowing my tyranny of the urgent to hold me hostage. **It really works!**

My prayer is for a sense of urgency to no longer feel such urgency and drama, but for simple blessings and true peace...just being and enjoying. Thank you...thank you!

Feeling Real Feelings

I remember how amazed I was, or perhaps *dumbfounded* is a better word, when I realized how hard it was for me to feel and express true feelings when I first went into treatment. This continued after treatment and happens even now at times. I usually think of myself as an artistic, deeply sensitive person, open to my emotions and feelings, helping others to be the same. But my isolation while medicating my most painful, secret feelings with alcohol for years atrophied my ability to feel honestly. Perhaps that is why one of my first assignments was to work through a book on denial.

I spent years intensely involved in growing a large, productive church, loving it for the most part, though always feeling I was on call twenty-four-seven. As I slowly burned out, I began more and more to numb my emotions, my pain, and my guilt through my abuse of alcohol, suffering its consequences.

But now, thankfully, *each week of sobriety allows true, inner feelings to drift back in healing ways,* even surprising ways. I am able to feel fears or emotions that date way back to parental abuse. I can now begin to better deal with those deep feelings in constructive, healthy ways.

One area that stirs up deep emotion and passion for me is art—any and all kinds. God has hardwired me to sense His presence through art. Recently I was held hostage, in the best sense of this phrase, by an amazing international story which has captivated, enthralled, and mesmerized me and the art world regarding the very real possibility of a lost Leonardo da Vinci painting that was discovered on October 14, 2009. And now, a couple years since the story broke, I've been able to order a book documenting and proving all the information that was first alleged relating to this seemingly impossible discovery. And how does this relate to recovery and growing?

The first time I read this amazing story, it became a strong reminder of my own recovery, but I will let you add your own recovery thoughts as art imitates life. Here is the story, from two different news sources, of the discovery of a lost painting by perhaps the greatest artist, sculpture, engineer, and inventor of all time, the true Renaissance man, Leonardo da Vinci.

Meet "La Bella Principessa," da Vinci's Lost Painting
Posted 10/14/2009 12:30 pm by Ron Hogan

Imagine walking into a gallery in New York City and buying a painting. An obscure work, thought to be 19th-century German. It's a well-made portrait, but nothing special. Then, after careful analysis and the lucky uncovering of a fingerprint, the truth is uncovered: for $19,000 you could have bought an original work of Leonardo da Vinci, the famed Renaissance artist, architect, inventor, and all-around creative genius.

Such is the tale of a painting now called "Profile of La Bella Principessa," a painting by da Vinci of Bianca Sforza, daughter of his patron Ludovico Sforza, the Duke of Milan. The painting dates from 1496 and is estimated to be worth several hundred million dollars. The work was painted on animal-skin vellum for the cover of a book of poetry dedicated to Bianca.

All the credit for saving the work goes to New York art dealer Peter Silverman, who first figured out that the painting wasn't 19th Century German, and who undertook the long and arduous process of figuring out just who painted the mystery girl. He consulted with experts from around the world, devoted hours of research into the students of da Vinci, and consulted with Lumière Technology in Paris for the high-tech spectral analysis that was icing on the cake. All that work and he doesn't even get to keep the painting!

I will use this story in my recovery life to say that the simplest little paintings, like everyday blessings that most people don't even see as valuable, become priceless treasures.

The former New York art gallery person, one Ms. Kate Glanz (see second article below), sold the painting to an art dealer who suspected the true origins and value of the painting. She stated, to paraphrase, "I did the best I could at the time given the knowledge and understanding I had of the painting." This statement strongly parallels what those of us in recovery from past abuse by our parent(s), and others, often say to assist us in our personal healing: "They did the best they could at the time for what they had." Whether this is true or not in a majority of cases, it's certainly true in a minority of them. And, like the more knowledgeable art dealer who bought the painting, there are always others out there, longer in the program, deeper in serenity and wisdom, waiting to share with us the treasure in what we may consider to be nice, but just average.

(ChattahBox) — *The fantasy of many an art collector has played out to a very happy ending. Recent history starts in 1998 with an auction at Christie's, New York, for a 13 x 9in picture, in chalk, pen and ink, catalogued as "German school, early 19th century," bought for $19,000 by Kate Ganz, a New York dealer. Unfortunately for Ms Ganz she sold it for about the same amount to Canadian-born Europe-based connoisseur Peter Silverman in 2007. Ganz had suggested that the portrait "may have been made by a German artist studying in Italy...based on paintings by Leonardo da Vinci."*

But when Mr Silverman first saw it, in a drawer, "my heart started to beat a million times a minute," he said. "I immediately thought this could be a Florentine artist. The idea of Leonardo came to me in a flash." A

Paris laboratory discovered that a fingerprint from the tip of an index or middle-finger, found on the top left of the picture, was "highly comparable" to one found on da Vinci's work St Jerome, which he painted early in his career when he did not have assistants, according to the Antiques Trade Gazette. Carbon dating and infrared analysis of the artist's technique were also consistent that it is almost certainly by Leonardo da Vinci, which makes it worth perhaps $150 million. Martin Kemp, Emeritus Professor of History of Art at the University of Oxford, who recently completed a book about the find (as yet unpublished) has rechristened the picture, sold as Young Girl in Profile in Renaissance Dress, as La Bella Principessa after identifying her, "by a process of elimination", as Bianca Sforza, daughter of Ludovico Sforza, Duke of Milan (1452–1508), and his mistress Bernardina de Corradis. He described the profile as "subtle to an inexpressible degree", as befits the artist best known for the Mona Lisa. Source: Times of London

From a Destructive Question to a Healing Exclamation

Even though I have attended a myriad of small-group meetings throughout my life, from workshops, think tanks, discerning groups, group counseling, and whatever other helpful group can be named, I have found none more powerful, honest, and life-changing than a simple AA meeting. Is that because it is often a life-and-death situation for many in attendance? One phrase sometimes heard is, "I have another drink in me, but not another recovery." Each week I am reminded again of this daily miracle.

Today, a young man came to our meeting, his first since getting out of treatment. He had gone through a "horrific mental, emotional, and spiritual battle" a few hours earlier, and was already planning on drinking that day. After calling everyone on the group's phone list, he found one person—a live voice—who agreed to bring him to the meeting. It was perfect timing, since the guy that brought him had just shared before me, saying, "I don't know what God's will is for my life." Then the newcomer shared, crediting that same man with saving his life twice during his sharing. I turned to him and whispered, "That's what God's will is for your life for this day." He smiled knowingly.

The newcomer, the most important person at the meeting, concluded by saying, "I had this amazing battle in my mind: before coming to the meeting I kept saying, 'Why am I not drinking today?' After coming to this meeting, my mind is saying '*This* is why I am not drinking today.'"

Thank you, God, for our amazing, practical, even miraculous 12-step program which changes our self-destructive questions into healing exclamations!

As Good As It Gets

I have found that the phrase "co-creators with God" gets thrown about when people are talking about a kind of New Age spirituality, or about feeling empowered, or about trying to live in more life-giving ways. I used to dislike the phrase because the context I heard it in seemed to replace God, or one's Higher Power, with the person themselves—they were making God in their own image. I don't think that way anymore. We are given the gift and power to create and re-create every day in so many ways, including the awesome and miraculous blessing of actually creating another human life! That is powerful co-creating with whatever it is we call God.

In reading one of my daily reflections, I realized that I am stuck in that unenviable place in life where I am between jobs. I have a basic, non-life-giving-while-you-wait kind of job that I can still be thankful for on some days, which I have been doing for almost four years. Other days I am thankful just to be able to survive it. But such employment has an element of enviableness as well. It can bless me in that it forces me to be patient and more present. I am learning that this may be as good as it gets. Tomorrow is promised to no one. Today is a special gift. So what am I waiting for? Because this position is not full time or permanent it affords me the opportunity to explore new areas of possible employment. I am trying to keep my head above water while living in the stress of waiting, wondering, not knowing, having few interviews, doubting myself, and so much more.

Part of today's reflection said to me: "Don't move too fast! You may not be at this place again, where you can actually choose your future and enjoy some precious time in between." I believe this, but I certainly need help with my unbelief. This sounds more like a "pie in the sky when I die" kind of thing, but I do believe I am where I should be, at least on most days.

I understand, it's about trust and acceptance and remembering the 12 Promises of AA that are daily working themselves out in my life. I believe my Higher Power has my address and phone number and is able to contact me quite easily in many ways on most days. He does this through people like you who are reading this book and who have given me many of these very words; people including my family and my personal recovery family.

My prayer is for peace and trust and presence, for not giving up on our dreams that allow us to find those places and professions which free us up to create and co-create for the best possible growth to ourselves and others.

Step 7

Humbly asked Him to remove our shortcomings.

Theme: Humility

The Garbage in Our Homes

Part-2

It's time to take the garbage from the side of the house to the curb on garbage day, knowing and believing that it will be picked up and taken away. Steps 2 and 3 consist of knowing and believing there is a cosmic garbage removal service out there, empowering us to find the garbage in our lives in Steps 4 and 5, and bring it out of our homes to the trash cans in Step 6.

But the garbage doesn't get from the side of our house to the street by itself—Step 7 involves doing all we can to bring that garbage to the curb by humbly asking Him to remove our shortcomings. What good does it do to bring the garbage from inside our house to the cans outside our house if we never bring it to the curb? We may avoid rodents within our home, but they will be swarming around the outside, trying to get inside. That's frightening! We may keep the creatures away from our family for a little longer, but we'll be affecting our neighbors by not dealing with the mess on the outside. Before long, there goes the neighborhood.

Dear Higher Power: Thank you for taking my mess away. Thank you for helping me in this process of recognizing my defects and giving them to You for proper disposal and the best of Your divine recycling service.

Hunchback Recovery Wings

I read a story recently that reminded me strongly of my personal recovery. It was about a mother who brought home a foster child with a deformity—a severe, crippling hunchback. The mother's son was the same age as the foster child. She took him aside and asked him not to talk about the other boy's deformity or make fun of him. A few days later the mother overheard her son talking to the boy, saying, "Do you know what that big hump on your back is for? It holds your wings that will help you fly!"

Wow! What a perfect recovery analogy! This story came back to me as I was walking this morning, just when I needed it most. It reminded me of perhaps the greatest blessing in my life: my very real Higher Power uses my worst deformities as strengths to help me fly above my self-imposed fears and worries. From this perspective, I gain an amazing healing view of living more in the present. This is a present filled with tension and doubt, as well as with future deformities, but one that I've been given new strength to wrestle with. I have been gifted with a present that forces me to be more honest with myself and more open to others.

I've known and taught for years that many of my greatest defects are my greatest strengths and gifts that have been pushed too far. Loving, leading, and working well with people can turn into manipulating people into fulfilling my desires or unmet needs. Deeply understanding spiritual truths can devolve into winning theological battles while losing the friendship war and being a poor witness for my faith. Enjoying solitude while using my creative gifts can lead to isolation, not sharing with others, not keeping in touch with my mentor/sponsor, or having few close friends. When I live into these defective traits, I refuel my worst fears, which leads me to a low-grade depression that in turn brings about the very defects that I have risen above in my recovery.

Another defect which haunts many addicts and alcoholics is the belief that "saying it is the same as doing it," or, "writing it to others publicly equals accomplishment." Wrong! But I am thankful that sharing with and receiving input from my recovery family over the years has become a key piece of my recovery puzzle. I am taking the next step, doing the next right thing. My wings are hidden in my deformed strengths. These steps are helping me slowly gain lift off! I am learning and re-learning to fly! *Thank you!*

And, I thank the One that makes my scars and my deformities beautiful and somehow uses them to help me fly.

Prison Bars

I liked an analogy from one of my readings this morning that likened our lives to looking out of prison bars. We all have prisons we're breaking out of, but some of us are still locked up within them. But what do we see from our prison bars—mud or stars?

I think my prison often consists of what I can't have, or of my inability to do what I want in life the way I could before hitting bottom, back when I had more money than time. I abused that freedom and those blessings were taken away-- *and that's just, the way, it is!* Be that as it may, a beautiful gift each day consists of choosing to see *stars* out of the bars and not *mud*. Was it Abraham Lincoln who said, "If you look for the bad in others, you will always find it?" The mud and the dirt are easy to find, but each person can be a star-studded gift to us if we look for the light in them.

As an artist, my favorite Expressionist artist is Vincent Van Gogh (born in 1853, exactly one hundred years before me!). He is often thought of as a tortured soul, experiencing long bouts of depression and eventually taking his own life at only thirty-seven years of age. Yet, one of his most productive periods of peace, contentment, and creativity was the year he spent in recovery in an asylum in France. He could have only seen the mud, but oh, the stars and the starry, starry nights he painted—they have inspired the world ever since. In fact, one could make an argument that it was because of Vincent's mental health issues that he was able to see and paint the world in a different, more colorful, artistic, and expressionistic way—not unlike our recovery and our recycling the muddy areas of our lives.

Yesterday was powerful and humbling. I received my three-year medallion during a large AA meeting from my sponsor, who has thirty-seven years of active sobriety. One of the gentlemen present was a man who has sixteen years of sobriety and someone I have admired since I came to what has become my home group. When his turn came to share, he looked over at my sponsor—who had been the counselor of his counselor in treatment, helping him with his blessed disease—and thanked him for being there. I thought, "That's amazing!" The miraculous, healing cycle continues.

The most powerful part of my home group is that it is made up of mostly older adults who collectively represent hundreds of years of sobriety. Yet each week, the van from the treatment facility brings a group of men and women from the seniors' program, most of whom have been sober for less than a month, and many for just a few days or weeks.

What makes this group so meaningful is that the seniors who come over see the seniors that have been coming back each week for decades. They see their peers smiling and laughing and letting them know that they themselves had sat in these same seats many years ago and were just like them. Here they are enjoying the sometimes fearful but hopeful beginnings of an incredible new life they had thought would never be possible. And, lest we forget, the newcomers strongly remind the old-timers of where they have come from and never want to go back to. One of them shared briefly and succinctly yesterday: "Hi, my name is Lewis and I'm an alcoholic. If I ever go back to drinking, I will die! I pass."

Thank you, Higher Power, for these sobering truths and walking miracles that help me choose, with Your strength, to see stars through the bars of my life!

"Does Anyone Need Some Special Time?"

One of the most important parts of our weekly AA meetings happens after the opening readings when the leader says, "Before we begin today's topic, is there anyone here that needs some special time to share something they may be struggling with in their recovery?" There is silence and waiting. In our group, someone speaks up about thirty percent of the time. More often than not it comes from women, who understand vulnerability as strength and not weakness.

The woman who spoke up this week was going through a traumatic experience that was paralyzing her emotionally. Her best friend was dying unexpectedly, at a young age. And, as so often happens, her boldness, bravery, and deep need for the strength of the group's sharing became the topic for the day. The chosen presenter quickly yielded to her need—another beautiful part of AA's healing format, and part of the reason why it has millions of members in similar groups spanning 173 countries.

This grieving newcomer was also new to the group in that she had been gone for a long time—in another great principle of AA, the newcomer is the most important person at the meeting. If I could make a video of the best part of an AA meeting (though I could not, since that would violate the anonymity and confidentiality of those present), it would have been made during this meeting. Almost all of the twenty-plus members present shared stories of their personal losses, not only telling our hurting guest that their hearts go out to her, but also offering Kleenex for her tears and an embrace for her fears. I was touched by what so many members shared, and began writing down some of what they said in my *Big Book*:

"I am so thankful that I was clean and sober when my loved one died, so I could not run away and isolate, self-destructing."

"It was so painful, but for the first time since I was sober, I could start to feel the pain from the beginning, and not put my recovery from the loss on hold by using again."

"Death cannot take away the gift that God gave me through that person."

"It's not the time we don't have with the person anymore, but the time we were blessed to have with them."

On and on and on came the healing sharing from personal tragedies. How blessed I was to be there and to be clean and sober myself to be able to take it all in.

---

*How beautiful that AA and NA can be honest, open,
and willing to face the hard questions in life,
unafraid of the tears, anger, silence, and
unanswerable questions in our complex lives and
out-of-control world. How powerful that there is a
Presence and Strength out there helping us know
that when we are weak,* It *is* strong! *From such
sharing on this day, it's easy to understand why
many have come to believe that such an unseen
power, deeply felt, is a strength made
perfect in our weakness.*

Autumn

*Winter is an etching, spring a watercolor,
summer an oil painting, and autumn
a mosaic of them all.*

~ Stanley Horowitz

Steps 8-9: Make Up

Steps 8 and 9 are about making up. I look at my broken relationships with God, with myself, and with others. I strive to see my part in how these unions became damaged. I ask my Higher Power what I can do to make amends and how to make up for the harm I've done in the past.

Step 8

Made a list of all persons we had harmed, and became willing to make amends to them all.

Theme: Forgiveness

Being Home for the Visit

I visited with a woman yesterday who was in intensive care for her methamphetamine addiction and suicide attempt. She was a broken woman. We had some things in common, and we talked about our difficulty with organized religion, our spirituality, our shame, and how deep pain from our addictions has produced life-changing consequences. Although she is in the infancy of her recovery process, barely able to feel hope for the future, she was able to smile. This was where she needed to be to get the help she needed. She told me that checking into the hospital voluntarily was her birthday gift to herself. To begin anew like this was such a huge step for her, and I told her how proud I was of her that she and her Higher Power were taking that step together.

I am thankful that since I am powerless my Higher Power gives me not only the desire and strength to make amends, but also the opportunities. I learned a long time ago that it's not about finding the right answer to some question; it's simply about not running away from the answer that is right in front of me.

God knows my address. He knows where I live, and He knows He is welcome. I'm trying to be home more often when He visits.

Setting the Prisoner Free

I was inspired, empowered, and centered again this morning as I read my daily reflections regarding the need for forgiveness of others and myself. It was sobering to understand that resentments are at the top of the list of things that contribute to relapse and to a state of non-growth. How healing it is to remember that I've been forgiven the million-dollar debt I could never repay so that I can forgive the five, ten, and twenty-dollar debts that others owe me. We close most AA meetings by holding hands and saying the Lord's Prayer, and that part about *"forgive us our trespasses as we forgive those who trespass against us"* is convincing in a healing way.

I remember a pivotal event in my life regarding deep healing through making amends with another—my father. I might call it an indirect amends, as it took place via my two brothers, one older and the other younger. We were at a family event many years ago and our father was not present though still alive before alcoholism cut his life short. We were talking about dad and his physical, verbal, and emotional abuse of us while we were growing up, his divorce of our mother, and his continued alcoholic behavior that left him an absent father from our lives. The more we talked together, processing, the more we were finally able to say, "How much longer are we going to allow dad to control our lives? We need to forgive him and move on." We were not saying that what he did was OK, but we were letting go of unrealistic expectations about what we needed our father to do. It wasn't going to happen. We all needed to get on with our lives.

The often-expressed truth about forgiveness came back to me during the weeks that followed that watershed experience with my brothers: *"To forgive another is to set a prisoner free and realize the prisoner was you."*

Although this was the first of many steps in letting go of my father's control over me, it was a great foundation to build upon.

Higher Power, thank you for reminding me how much you love me and have forgiven me. Empower me to love and forgive others by giving me the desire to desire it. Please remind me often, as I so quickly forget.

Forgiveness Needed for Deep Healing

I was reminded indirectly but very specifically this morning about the need of forgiveness in my personal life for deep, ongoing healing. While making my rounds as a hospital chaplaincy intern, I visited a victim of an alcohol-related hit-and-run accident. The patient had specified no religion. I prayed with her, thanking God that she was not injured more seriously. After my prayer, she blurted out that I needed to be praying for the woman that had hit her and driven away, because "she *really* needs it!"

Her words caught me off-guard, but I was able to reply, "You're right! I should have included her in my prayer, and I will pray for her. She's going to need it in the coming days and will have to work on forgiveness issues for herself and others." I was able to mention to the patient, her mom, and her aunt that perhaps they too will have to work on their forgiveness issues for further healing from their anger against the woman who had done such a crazy, dangerous, life-threatening thing.

"No religion" had been specified by this patient, but she shared a very spiritual truth with me, and now I pass it on to you. As I sit here thinking about this hours-old incident, I realize how important ongoing forgiveness of myself and others continues to be in my own life and personal recovery. I know this is obvious and I hear it all the time in meetings from my sponsor and recovery friends, but it doesn't always sink in until just the right moment—until a time like this.

I'm giving thanks to my Higher Power this morning for His simple truths about forgiveness and how I can apply them today to my life, and for keeping the patient I visited from worse injury. Yet, more to the point, I pray for the woman who left the scene of the crime while under the influence, and for how this will all play out in her life, and, hopefully, in her recovery.

Miraculous Forgiveness

Forgiveness is always miraculous, but the following true story from a German concentration camp in postwar recovery illustrates the best of what true forgiveness is all about. Corrie ten Boom, the Dutch Christian Holocaust survivor who helped many Jews escape the Nazis during World War II, shared this transformational story about a Nazi officer and her personal experience of amazing grace.

IT WAS IN A CHURCH in Munich where I was speaking in 1947 that I saw him—a balding heavyset man in a gray overcoat, a brown felt hat clutched between his hands. One moment I saw the overcoat and the brown hat, the next, a blue uniform and a visored cap with its skull and crossbones.

Memories of the concentration camp came back with a rush: the huge room with its harsh overhead lights, the pathetic pile of dresses and shoes in the center of the floor, the shame of walking naked past this man. I could see my sister's frail form ahead of me, ribs sharp beneath the parchment of skin.

Betsie and I had been arrested for concealing Jews in our home during the Nazi occupation of Holland. This man had been a guard at Ravensbruck concentration camp where we were sent.

Now he was in front of me, hand thrust out: "A fine message, Fraulein! How good it is to know that, as you say, all our sins are at the bottom of the sea!"

It was the first time since my release that I had been face to face with one of my captors and my blood seemed to freeze.

"You mentioned Ravensbruck in your talk," he was saying. "I was a guard there. But since that time," he went on, "I have become a Christian. I know that God has forgiven me for the cruel things I did there, but I would like to hear it from your lips as well, Fraulein"—again the hand came out—"will you forgive me?"

And I stood there—and could not. Betsie had died in that place—could he erase her slow terrible death simply for the asking?

It could not have been many seconds that he stood there, hand held out, but to me it seemed hours as I wrestled with the most difficult thing I had ever had to do.

For I had to do it—I knew that. The message that God forgives has a prior condition: that we forgive those who have injured us. "If you do not forgive men their trespasses," Jesus says, "neither will your Father in Heaven forgive your trespasses."

Still I stood there with the coldness clutching my heart. But forgiveness is an act of the will, and the will can function regardless of the temperature of the heart. "Jesus, help me!" I prayed silently. "I can lift my hand. I can do that much. You supply the feeling."

And so woodenly, mechanically, I thrust my hand into the one stretched out to me. And as I did, an incredible thing took place. The current started in my shoulder, raced down my arm, sprang into our joined hands. And then this gelling warmth seemed to flood my whole being, bringing tears to my eyes. "I forgive you, brother!" I cried. "With all my heart!"

For a long moment we grasped each other's hands, the former guard and former prisoner. I had never known God's love so intensely as I did then.

+   +   +

Suck It Up! - Deal With It

I've been hearing those competing "voices" in my head and heart lately—perhaps in direct proportion to how long and draining my week has been and how recently I've been to a meeting, called my sponsor, prayed, and practiced the basics of a simple program that is not easy. One voice feels sorry for myself, pities me, and brings out thoughts like "this isn't fair or you don't deserve these kinds of feelings."

The other voice is quite strong and overly direct with little or no sympathy: "Deal with it!" "Suck it up!" I'm thinking, "That's not very nice. Suck it up?!" But that voice goes on trying to allow gratitude to emerge: "Look at all your blessings! Look how far you've come! Would you prefer to be dead or paralyzed from your last drink when you destroyed your motorcycle? What if you had had a passenger with you, or had run into another car?"

Steps 8 and 9 are about getting rid of our character defects though making amends. Often times we need to *just do it.* This relates well to sucking up our pride, humbling ourselves through the strength of our Higher Power.

The "What-ifs" haunt me, but are good reality therapy. How easily I could have killed someone during my last binge when I had a blackout or knock-out and came to consciousness in a ditch with ambulance lights flashing and sirens blaring! I was a bloody mess—a rag doll flung across the highway and into the ditch, totally unconscious, covered with lacerations and with road rash that was exposed through torn, bleeding clothes.

Recovery is all about growing up, and part of that growth certainly includes "sucking it up." It reminds me of a statement someone made at my AA meeting this week: "I used to complain about my shoes until I met a person who had no feet." I realize again in this roller-coaster recovery journey that I can be bitter or better, and the difference depends on the letter "I"—me, and my Higher Power's empowerment in my powerlessness!

So, Brother Kenny, count your blessings,
and suck it up! Deal with it—and be thankful!

Surrender and Submission

One of my recovery readings this morning talked about surrender, and it reminded me of an AA meeting I attended this week. The presenter said something that the *Big Book* often echoes: "I don't worry so much about drinking, but I have to deal with my sobriety every day." That is a strong parallel to the often-heard adage "I don't have a drinking problem, but I have a living problem." This recovery truth is also related to "Wherever I go, I take myself with me." We can lament our circumstances all we want, lacking mature acceptance as we play the blame game, and can continue to take ourselves with us wherever we go. Nothing changes, especially not our ongoing "slip-slid'n-away."

At the risk of oversimplification, everyone in the world has problems, and everyone deals with these problems in different ways—some healthy, some unhealthy. Those of us who are alcoholics and addicts deal with the pain from our problems by self-medicating with alcohol and drugs. Others delve into a variety of self-destructive acts through eating too little or too much, working themselves to death, gambling, sex—you name it! There is an unhealthy addiction for everyone. There is a drug of choice for everyone out there to assist them in surviving, though not for long. Surviving, just holding our head above water, is not thriving.

There is only *one solution* to get at the foundation of healing: *surrender and submission.* It's giving up! It's submitting to a Higher Authority as we finally realized our authority was bankrupt. Letting go, letting God. It's a simple solution, but it may be the hardest thing we ever do. That's the bad news, and the really bad news is that this may be something we can never do! But thank God for some good news: Only a power greater than ourselves can do *in* us and *through* us what we can never do on our own. That very power gives us the power to surrender and to submit.

My reading reminded me of a phrase I have often heard when visiting prisons and jails, shared joyfully with us by recovering inmates. They have declared, "I am freer in prison, growing in my faith and recovery, than I could ever have been on the outside." There is a strong parallel here to living the sober life even within the prison walls of our lives, with daily temptations and the struggle to control our addictive personalities. This lifestyle is impossible, I believe, outside of living our faith through the 12-Step program or something very close to it. My Higher Power is gracious, and when I have no power, when I can only surrender and submit, it is then that I become a part of the true bedrock of recovery. I can choose to accept it or not. I can choose to be "God" myself, or take the power given to me and surrender. I am powerless to heal myself, and the only power I have is from the Great Healer, the One who transforms us from the walking wounded to the wounded healer.

With the amazing grace given me, I can choose
self-destruction and annihilation, or I can
take the power given to me and surrender.
Is there really a choice?

Ready, FIRE! Aim.

I was inspired by one of my readings this morning which talked about breaking through the paralysis of our disease and taking action, moving forward, just doing it, even if it is with small steps, baby steps, and one step at a time. How quickly we can get stuck in the muck and mire of feeling lost, not knowing what to do. We become afraid to do anything, thinking it might be wrong, letting our fears overwhelm us and just do the "comfortable thing," which is nothing—one step forward, two steps back!

Truth: Not making amends, allowing resentments to fester and grow, is a deep cause of sobriety-paralysis.

I've always liked the phrase "Ready, Fire! Aim." There comes a time to stop playing around spending too much time aiming, trying to do it perfectly as our distant prey wanders away—a once-in-a-lifetime opportunity missed! There comes a time to *just do it*, allowing our serenity prayer to flow through us, believing we are receiving the wisdom to know the difference and the power to act on it.

Action, moving forward, stepping out, and taking risks have never been a problem for me; they come easily, almost too easily, and I've often jumped out too quickly and impetuously. Yet other times, especially now during my steady, growing recovery, I am learning to not just stand there but to do something. I am slowly gaining the wisdom and discernment to not only know the difference, but to also *act* on that knowledge. It may not be an *either/or*, but a *both/and* if the divine timing is right.

In my early recovery I did anything but move forward. I was paralyzed with fear, afraid to go to a meeting in our small town, afraid of the future, afraid of being found out, afraid and paralyzed by the humiliation, shame, and guilt of it all. There are still times during the week that I fight these fears. I am only making slow progress, but I am making progress. God's amazing grace and unconditional love is working through *everything* in my life, not just the things I think most right or consider to be my best decisions. He knows my frame. He knows I'm dust. Yet I am His dust; I'm clay in the Master Potter's hands, being created, re-created, and transformed in His large, loving, strong hands.

The Loving Father

With one of my usernames on a recovery blog site being "prodigal returned," I cannot *not* comment on today's *Twenty-Four Hours A Day* reflection. Yes, I have squandered my Father's resources, indulged in "riotous living" and ended up sleeping with the pigs, longing to go home, not even worthy to be called a son, but just wanting a place to call home. Certainly one of my favorite sections in Scripture is this portion in the Gospel of Luke, chapter 15. This solid-gold chapter includes three "lost but found" parables about the lost sheep, the lost coin, and the lost son.

One of the most difficult things we will ever do in recovery, and in life, is to humble ourselves, push away our pride, and deal with our resentments by making amends. The only way we can truly do that is to remember where we have come from. We can forgive another and ask for forgiveness because we have been forgiven.

Thankfully, and grace-fully, these words are not so much about the lost son as about the loving father, who welcomed his ragged, smelly son home after watching and waiting for him for so long. It was right that he should celebrate and have a huge feast because his son, who was spiritually dead, is now alive! He was lost and is now found! It doesn't matter that his son's self-righteous older brother hated him and could not understand such unconditional love.

In 12-Step language, we could say that the older brother still has not completed Step 1, as he is failing to realize his own life is unmanageable and out of control through his prejudice and self-righteousness. He cannot move on to Steps 2 and 3 and come to know a God who loves him no matter what he's done or where he's been sleeping. The loving father understands, forgives, heals, and welcomes his resurrected son home.

AA Thought for the Day

The Prodigal Son "took his journey into a far country and wasted his substance with riotous living." That's what we alcoholics do. We waste our substance with riotous living. "When he came to himself, he said: "I will arise and go to my father." That's what you do in AA. You come to yourself. Your alcoholic self is not your real self. Your sane, sober, respectable self is your real self. That's why we alcoholics are so happy in AA.

Have I come to myself?

Step 9

Made direct amends to such people wherever possible, except when to do so would injure them or others.

Theme: Justice

Being the Change

Since it's easier to talk about making amends other than my own, let me begin by sharing an amazing experience that blew me away a few years ago. I left my car parked outside my house with the keys in it because I was planning to drive it into the garage later, but then went to bed and forgot about it. The next morning my car was gone. The police and my insurance agent thought for sure that my teenage kids had taken it, but I had already investigated that angle, and they both had good alibis. The next day the police called and said they had found my car. It was ninety miles away, out of gas, and undamaged. I found a way to bring it home.

About a year later I received a letter in the mail from a young teenage girl who was "serving time" in an adolescent home down the path from our home. She said that she had been walking down the trail with her friend, saw my car with the keys in it, and felt powerless not to take it. Those were her words, not mine. She wrote her letter to me as her amends for stealing my vehicle. She even included her full name and address. I wrote her back, thanking her for being honest and willing to give her name and share her "acting out." I never heard from her again, but I didn't need to. What she did initially is part of our disease; what she did in working this step is part of her recovery.

It is easier to share another person's story, but because of the boldness and honesty of others around me, I am increasingly able to share my own. Sometimes I have little or no choice in the matter, as I am forced to do so—busted! One such incident happened at the church I began in our home, which grew to over 700 members in the fifteen years I served as its pastor. After my last drink, my accident, and all the publicity surrounding it, I needed to make public amends. As part of my amends, I wrote a heartfelt and honest letter to all the members of the church. I also stood up (or kneeled) in front of them all on a Sunday morning, in all three worship services, having hands laid on me by the associate pastor and elders, confessing my sins and receiving the forgiveness of all.

This was one of the most difficult, humbling, and shameful events I have ever participated in. It was also the beginning of my healing process, which involved inpatient treatment, then a year of aftercare involving outpatient therapy, counseling, and two AA meetings a week. I have never stopped attending those meetings and they have taught me a new way of daily living. I am still in the process of healing after two and a half years. I have chosen to face the pain by embracing it and growing through it, rather than running away by isolating, self-medicating, or choosing a geographical escape by moving out of town.

Making direct amends may be the most difficult thing we will ever do, but may also be the most life-changing. I receive courage and strength in believing that my Higher Power gave me the ability and continues to give me the desire to make needed amends. I believe He orchestrates all the events in my life to push me further along in my spiritual journey.

I first shared this story with God, myself, and another human being in my Fourth and Fifth Steps; then with my sponsor, therapist, wife, and weekly groups early in my recovery; and now with all of you who read these heartfelt words. My hope is they will contribute toward ongoing amends and healing in your own lives when needed, and when you are ready and able with God's strength to do so.

"Be the change you want to see in the world."

—Mahatma Gandhi

Reclaiming Our Golf Courses

Part-1

I came home from work late last night after a very long, hard, and draining week. As usual, I took my dog Nikki to the private golf course at the end of our street's cul-de-sac, walking up the hill and jumping over the fence. I have enjoyed this ritual from November through April for the past twenty-three years, and the past twelve with Nikki. It felt good and centering to sit on the edge of one of the great sand traps in the dark, with the almost-full moon peeking out mysteriously from the clouds. I thought, "How can I let go of the worst of this week and internalize the best of it?"

Thinking of this question, the words "Thank you" kept coming to mind. I heard myself saying "Thank you, thank you, thank you" out loud. I realized that this emerging thankfulness was my way of decompressing from the week, keeping me from getting the "burnout bends" that I learned about in scuba training. In my haste and enthusiasm, I often try to swim to the surface more quickly than my body can adjust to the pressure of all that this week threw at me.

Therefore, I am reclaiming the golf course. It's not my golf course—in fact I've been told that in not so many words—sometimes angry words—by a snooty neighbor who thinks he owns it and who actually patrols it. Like many people in the area, he has spent thousands of dollars to join this private country club, and is required to $pend a certain amount monthly in the clubhouse and restaurant as part of their membership. I could never afford that, especially after losing my very good job a couple years ago due to my alcoholism and its consequences.

I am now just scraping by, very thankful to be able to make our house payments. My amazing, loving wife did not leave me but paid the price by getting a full-time job to make ends meet. I still remember her words through tears at those brutal, weekly family days during my inpatient treatment: "I'm willing to go through the pain now if it will make for a stronger marriage later." That's amazing grace and slow, steady healing. Thanks honey; I could not be where I am, or where we are together, without your unconditional love that reflects God's love to me.

This special healing helped me in many areas—even in letting go of my resentment of my snooty neighbor. We can at least wave at each other now, though I still don't know his name. I can stay off the course from May through October, avoiding the members' wrath. But like our recovery lives, it's time now to reclaim it.

What are the golf courses in your life, places of healing and strength, which are waiting to be reclaimed?

Thank you, God, for saving me from myself.
Thank you for helping me reclaim the golf courses
of my life, those special places that enlarge my life,
helping me be open to your presence working
through your creation. Help me be ready for
and open to encounters with others that
may need my amends.

Reclaiming Our Golf Courses

Part-2

As Nikki and I left on our slow jog this morning, I thought of taking my digital camera but quickly rejected that idea since it was a cloudy, overcast day. "There could not be much beauty with such little sunlight," I thought. I cut over to the beautiful, manicured golf course near our home, and then jogged up and down the hill that sweeps along the mighty Mississippi River. There, in full view up in a leafless tree, sat two huge bald eagles. One was large, the other very large. They were just sitting there with their magnificent features, craning their elegant white heads to see what Nikki and I were up to. Amazing! Most often I cannot get within a block of these majestic creatures, whose keen eyesight can spot rodents a mile away.

If I had taken my camera, you would now be looking at exactly what we saw—even better, a zoomed-in view. Damn! I see eagles soaring on occasion by the river, but never two of them sitting in a tree just a few yards away. I thought for Nikki's safety at first. Two of those eagles, working in tandem, could perhaps have had the strength to swoop down the open fairway and grab her with their mighty talons, taking her away for a great feast with their eaglets. I thought, "That would be a great picture if it happened—a Kodak moment—but I forgot my camera!" I let go of the sick humor and my brief fear of losing Nikki, wanting to stay in the magic of the moment.

I stopped, prayed, gave thanks, and decided to walk slowly toward the eagles. I had only walked a few yards when the not-so-huge one gave out a piercing cry, flexed its mighty wings and floated off the branch, swooping down the river to an island tree a few hundred yards downstream. The other just sat there as I got closer and closer, then it too swooped away, flying effortlessly in all its splendor. Those would have been amazing pictures. I'm glad I can still see them in my mind's eye and heart.

I missed the photograph, but caught much more. Those eagles were my Higher Power's sign this day to help me reclaim this golf course for the next six months, knowing it will be an important part of my sober activity, amidst high snowdrifts and beautiful glistening river panoramas. I learned that both eagles had names—a number of blessed names: *grace* and *glory*, *peace* and *serenity*, *forgiveness* and *healing*, *passion* and *love*—those are God's healing gifts to me in my recovery.

These are God's gifts to all of us in recovery; by His amazing grace we are receiving them—sometimes quickly, sometimes slowly. They will *always* materialize as we receive the daily strength to work for them.

I learned today that there can be great beauty with little sunlight.

New-Old Signs In My Life

This morning I read a new sign that Jim, an amazing elderly friend, had written and was displaying over his workbench:

Higher Power, help me get to know your voice so that I can stay in the safety of your fold. Thank you for your unfailing and faithful love.

I liked that, but I liked the one below it even better:

Whatever you are doing, find God in it. Our resources for devotions are as varied as our imaginations.

This relates to one of the most powerful action truths in my life of recovery:

Find out what God is doing and jump into the middle of it.

I love this! While listening to and inwardly digesting the books of writer and spiritual teacher Eckhart Tolle, *The Art of Presence* and *The Power of Now*, I was inspired by his thoughts regarding my own Higher Power. Tolle wrote about how to manage an encounter with someone whom we have a history of conflict and a number of unresolved issues relating to forgiveness. This is not unlike Steps Eight and Nine and the need to make amends with those individuals. Tolle taught of our response to be as much in the present with the offenders as we possibly can, treating them as if there is no history between us. Our goal: to be with them as if we were with someone we just met, a new friend or acquaintance.

Those thoughts created a kind of epiphany for me about my Higher Power. I remember that one of my names for God, as I understand God, is "I AM." In other words, my God is totally and always in the present with me—there is no past record of sins and wrongs! I am not saying there are no consequences for my past actions—I am living with them. What I am saying is that my understanding of God is often way too small:

My God is God and graciously chooses to forget my destructive past, removing it as far as the east is from the west. I have always believed that. But it helps me personally to know that He is the total I AM, and loves me deeply and completely in the present moment—that's all there is!

That's all there is…and that's all there ever will be; not yesterday, not tomorrow, just ***now***. And perhaps the most important outcome of this realization is to believe I can offer the same love and forgiveness to my enemies.

Higher Power, thank you for modeling and empowering me to extend the same love and forgiveness to others as You have to me. Help me be present with them as You are with me.

Semi-solid Gifts

It's time to dog-sit a bit, not for Nikki, the amazing, happy, beautiful Pomeranian that we've been blessed with for over nine years, but with her little niece Sasha. We are dog-sitting for the week while our daughter goes on vacation with her husband to meet her in-laws in Kentucky, wanting to make a good first impression.

Sasha is a really cute, wild, yappy puppy with catlike tendencies. She's really fun, even though on her first morning at our house she left a semi-solid gift on our basement floor instead of doing any of her business outdoors on our walk together. She was probably just marking her territory. Puppies are like that. And how does this relate to recovery?

- All life is recovery.

- How great it is to enjoy such gifts in a sober state, not angrily wanting to make a hat out of the dog.

- A good self-worth-builder in that often used and very appropriate prayer: *God, make me into the person my dog thinks I am.*

- In my sober-serenity state, I have much less chance than I used to have of leaving semi-solid gifts by way of self-destructive behavior!

*Thank you God for slowly but surely making me
into the kind of person my dog thinks I am. Peace
to you puppies out there this day as we keep
growing in good, strong, solid
(not semi-solid) recovery!*

Not Wasting Away Again in Margaritaville

Today's topics at my AA meetings were just what the doctor ordered: "Honesty" and "Forgiveness." The honesty topic centered on taking responsibility for the consequences of our disease—our acting out and hurting others—and on not playing the typical blame game in response.

It reminded me of the healing progression in Jimmy Buffett's classic song "Wasting Away Again In Margaritaville." Though he may be under the influence of that frozen concoction, or he may be sobering up, he feels bad and starts pondering his predicament before he cranks up the blender again.

His song progression is:

1. *I can't blame the woman; in fact, it's nobody's fault.*
2. *Hell, it could be my fault.*
3. *I know—it's my own damn fault!*

He even repeats it again! Not bad for living in Margaritaville; or St. Cloud, Minnesota; or Anytown, USA!

The topic of forgiveness was highlighted by the often quoted but difficult-to-practice words of daily wisdom from page 552 in the *Big Book of Alcoholics Anonymous,* Fourth Edition, as a member named Joanne shared what had worked in her life:

If you have a resentment you want to be free of, if you will pray for the person or the thing that you resent, you will be free. If you will ask in prayer for everything you want for yourself to be given to them, you will be free. Ask for their health, their prosperity, their happiness, and you will be free. Even when you don't really want it for them and your prayers are only words and you don't mean it, go ahead and do it anyway. Do it every day for two weeks, and you will find you have come to mean it and to want it for them, and you will realize that where you used to feel bitterness and resentment and hatred, you now feel compassionate understanding and love."

These well-worn words are perhaps a bit simplistic for victims of sexual, emotional, physical, and other kinds of abuse, but certainly are a healing place to begin. We ask our God as we understand God, to work that healing according to his will and amazing grace.

In summary, I can relate to all this in a sober way: I can use my blender to make a non-alcoholic smoothie this morning, learning that I can have fun with sober activities! ..... I also need to go buy another pair of flip-flops!

191

Winter

In the depths of winter, I finally learned that within me lay an invincible summer.

—Albert Camus

Winter! How do you survive it? You get out into it and enjoy it! How do you survive a cold, deep winter? How do you survive a life of cold, hard, recovery? You get out into it! You learn how to dress in layers, layers of the healing 12 Steps! You immerse yourself in meetings, and sharing the message! You take giant wintry steps forward!

Step 10

Continued to take personal inventory and when we were wrong promptly admitted it.

Theme: Perseverence

Steps 10-12: Keep Up

"Stepping Back From It"
Or
"Stepping In It!"

"Shit Happens!" ~ **Forrest Gump**

I had one of those "It could have been avoided" teachable moments this morning—totally avoidable if I had listened to the two prophetesses sent to me in as many days. The first was my wife, Joan. We are dog-sitting our adorable, ear-splitting-barking Pomeranian puppy Sasha. Unlike her aunt Nikki, who does her business on the path, Sasha likes our yard. Yesterday I took her out and was happy she went "so much," so I shared the good news with Joan. Joan's immediate response was, "Did you clean it up with the shovel?" I said, "No, but I will."

The second prophetess was my cousin Heidi, who just this morning responded to a reflection I sent out about not sweating the petty things (or is it "not petting the sweaty things"?). Heidi prophesied by writing: *Indeed it's easy to get wrapped up in miniscule issues that seem to block out the light of the day. I keep trying to "step back" before I "step in it"!*

Okay, I copy that. "He who has ears to hear, let him hear!" But since I just turned fifty-seven, I think my hearing is going. Or is it procrastination? Denial? Brain damage? (I can hear well enough to detect a faint voice saying "Ken, it's all of the above!") So, I got Sasha up an hour ago, took her immediately outside to do her business. As I stood there, I felt something moist, soft, and mushy under my right bare foot. Yes, you guessed it, and it felt like it wasn't from yesterday!

In summary: "If I don't step back from all the 'shit' in my life, I will step in it!" Or, more appropriate in our recovery, "If we don't clean up our messes from yesterday, we will step in them today!"

Leaky Air Mattress

Well, I've got some bad news, some really bad news, and some good news. Which, before I continue, reminds me of a joke?

This guy is feeling really sick. He goes to his doctor and has some tests done. The doctor calls him back with the results, saying, "I don't know how to say this, but I've got some bad news, and some really bad news."

The guy says, "Wow, Doc, I don't know what to say, but give me the bad news first."

"Well," the doc says, "your tests came back and you have a terminal illness...and...you only have twenty-four hours to live!"

"Wow! That's terrible! What could be the really bad news?!"

"Well," the doc says, "I tried calling you yesterday!"

My actual bad news from yesterday was that, against the advice of my higher power—not God, but my wife—I bought the Cadillac of air mattresses, on sale no less, for only $84.00! It is a beauty, queen-sized, pump included, with a nice carrying case. When I called my wife from the store she said, "But I bought our last one that worked great for only $35.00." But I persisted, bought it, took it home, filled it up, and it leaked. Since all sales were final, I threw away the receipt—my second mistake.

I thought I could go back to the store today, plead my case with the manager, and at least get another receipt from him that I could send to the manufacturer. I was told on the phone today by the corporate office that there is a one-year guarantee *if* you include the receipt! That's the bad news.

The really bad news is that the store wasn't kidding when they said they were closing! When I went there today, it was all locked up—out of business—closed! Talk about feeling powerless!

But there is some good news: I finally took the original pump that came with the mattress, charged it for twenty-four hours and attached it to the limping mattress. It instantly inflated way beyond what my old pump, not designed for this mattress, had done. It's been twenty-four hours and the mattress is still completely full and not leaking! I haven't slept on it yet, but there's hope.

And what does this have to do with anyone's recovery? Well, you can draw your own conclusions, but for starters, I know I'm an airhead—I already heard that phrase from a couple of people I shared my story with. I also heard last night at home, "Always keep receipts!" My response was, "Don't you think I know that?" But this experience reminds me so much of AA and my recovery: keep it simple, follow directions, practice the 12 Steps, go to meetings, meet with my sponsor, be open to having a sponsee, pray, take it one day at a time, "Suit Up, Show Up, Shut Up," and many more well-worn, time-tested tools that our amazing program of recovery gives us on a daily basis.

Don't be your own Higher Power! Don't do your own thing; it won't work. Or it might work for a while but you'll wake up on the hard floor of your tent which is your leaking, self-willed life! That doesn't work anymore—especially since you have burned all your bridges. The store is closed, out of business; and you have no receipts, nothing to show for it, only *consequences!*—I hate that word!

This experience also reminds me of the heart of this book and my recovery life:

My Higher Power is not interested in making me into some Humpty Dumpty person, putting me back together the way I used to be. He wants to take all the broken pieces of my life that I'm willing and able to give Him at this time and make a brand-new creation, a new sculpture--something I could never become if I had never been broken.

I believe this on most days, but often add this faith statement: "Lord, help my unbelief!"

Resurrection, Surfing, Recovery

Question one: "What do resurrection, surfing, and recovery have in common?"

❖ Nothing, but they were all a part of my past week.

❖ Everything, they are pieces of my daily recovery.

Question two: "What is the best to get into great physical shape and have extreme fun while you're doing it?

❖ Surfing, body surfing, boogie boarding, and just playing in the ocean's healing waters—hydrotherapy at its best.

❖ Interpersonal, playful, physical re-lationships (i.e. making love; but that's a whole other blog entry and perhaps contains too many triggers for me to do it justice at this time).

My wife and I were blessed to be able to vacation in Florida's hot sun, sand, and surf following the long Lenten season, Holy Week, and Easter Sunday. We escaped the almost twelve inches of snow in central Minnesota. This adventurous vacation reminded me of what I've known and loved for so long about the mysterious healing ocean waters we enjoyed off Florida's east coast:

There's only one way to catch a wave, whether it's with your body or board, and that's by moving as fast as the wave is moving so it catches you and takes you. If you don't, you will miss it; then the wave will either wash over you or take you down, and sometimes waaaaaaay down.

We watched one guy this week trying to get his board out to where he could surf. After an hour of trying, he gave up. He reminded us of the Tom Hanks character in the movie *Castaway* who was never able to make it beyond the crashing waves until he got the extra winged wind power to break out of his prison like island towards home, experiencing his new, strange, painful, resurrected life.

Here is the daily resurrection power available to all of us in recovery as we work the program-- the 12 Steps, sponsors, meetings, sponsees, daily readings--all serving as that extra set of wings to help us break free, moving beyond our imprisoned environment. And once we do, though re-entering this life may be strangely painful, it can ultimately be a powerful, resurrected life. As we live out our 12-Step program of active sobriety we will hear ourselves screaming in no time:

"LOOK, I'M SURFING! I REALLY CAN DO IT!" It IS possible! Just think of all the possibilities ahead! Just think what great physical, emotional, mental, and spiritual shape we will be growing in! *"Surf's up!!"* I'm there! We're there!!!

Step 11

Sought through prayer and meditation to improve our conscious contact with God, as we understood Him, praying only for knowledge of His will for us and the power to carry that out.

Theme: Spirituality

People often say that God speaks to them when they take long walks, retreats, or camping trips, and just get away from the rat race. I think it is then, in nature's pregnant silences, that we can finally...hear His voice.

Living in the Now—Not Yet!

Here is a great truth I believe: *We are going to live forever and our eternal relationship with the Divine begins now and goes on forever!* By the grace of our Higher Power, we don't have to somehow hope to sneak in the back door of Heaven, whatever you understand Heaven to be in this life and in the next.

Heaven begins now and goes on forever!

I haven't found much certainty about this truth on the part of most spiritual people I meet, nor in much of the spiritual literature I have read—it's one of the best-kept secrets. Yet this truth is one of the joys of true recovery and spirituality.

There is much talk of waiting, waiting, waiting for something better. I fully understand this sentiment, being in my nineteenth month of sobriety and the hell of all the consequences of use, misuse, and abuse. *But today is all we have.* As the title of the movie states, this might be *As Good As It Gets*. The present, right now, is all we have. What if today is our last day on earth?

From much of my reading and interacting with others over the decades, there are many well-meaning words out there, but they often seem to me like pie in the sky when you die, a product of fear of aging and death. This is sad, since the great truth in recovery and healing—and living each day with the grace given us—is that we are living in the "now, not yet." We have a divine relationship with our Higher Power and have the hope and promise of eternal life—it's a done deal—but we are not there yet. We often experience "previews of coming attractions" in the spiritual realm. This truth reminds me of one of my favorite spirituals, "One Day Jesus Will Call My Name," by Phil McHugh.

> *One day Jesus will call my name,*
> *As days go by, I hope I don't stay the same,*
> *I wanna get so close to Him,*
> *That it's no big change,*
> *On that day when Jesus calls my name.*

In a growing relationship with our Higher Power, death is only a shadow. The best-known Psalm reads, "Yea, though I walk through the valley of the shadow of death, I will fear no evil for thou art with me."(23) I believe, along with many others, that our last breath on earth is our first breath in heaven. Death simply means stepping across the line into what's really real, and that reality begins *now*.

In his book *The Great Divorce*, C.S. Lewis powerfully illustrates this truth when he writes about a bus coming from Earth to Heaven, carrying mortals who have not yet been "translated." They try getting out of the bus in Heaven, and the brilliance of the place blinds them. They attempt to walk on the beautiful leaded-crystal grass and it hurts their feet. The residents of Heaven are called "the solid people," and they walk freely through the grass, fully enjoying the glorious present. The earthlings, held hostage on the bus, are like shifting shadows that are unable to withstand the heavenly glory that is Heaven's everyday reality.

We live in the now, not yet. This Now is a foretaste of Heaven, though it is often obscured when we become trapped in our daily, mundane existence, unable to see the eternal forest because of earthly trees. We will live forever. Now, in this reality, we don't have to be afraid of death—it's been defeated and becomes our means of transportation whenever we step across that line. Of course, none of us wants to suffer, and I believe we will only suffer according to the measure of faith we've been given. Though this can be an overworked axiom shared too freely with people who are suffering, I believe our Higher Power will not give us more than we can bear, but with the suffering will provide a means of escape and give us the ability to not only survive but also thrive.

Therefore, it's not just "pie in the sky when we die." We don't have to mourn and wait and worry and hope. We can realize that when this earthly tent we live in is destroyed, we have a heavenly, eternal home, not built by human hands. To help us slowly understand this truth, we have been given the Spirit, as a down payment, guaranteeing all that is to come (2 Cor. 5:1-5). How awesome! What a gift! "Lord, I believe; help my unbelief."

_____

+ My Amazing Mother +

At the former church I served, every fifth Sunday of the month became a time of public sharing. There was no liturgy or sermon, just lots of good music. Anyone could come forward and share the way they felt their Higher Power was working in their lives. I came forward and said to the large congregation, "I have a secret to share with you. I haven't told anyone this, but this is the day I need to share it with you." It was very quiet. I said slowly,

"Some of the best years of my life have been spent in the arms of another man's wife!"

It got even quieter. I could tell I had gotten the attention of some of the church elders, and no one was sleeping. But it was Mother's Day that Sunday, and I just looked at everyone and said,

"That's my mother! Happy Mother's Day!"

Yes, some of the best years of my life have truly been spent in the arms of another man's wife—the loving arms of my amazing mother. So much of my current recovery life is aided and abetted by the unceasing prayers of my prayer-warrior mother. Some of the best years of her life were spent married to my father before his drinking increased, before he began violently abusing her and his five children. When I was seven years old, my father ran off with another woman; my mother hit her bottom, almost giving up, going through a deep depression.

But it was her children, her faith, and the encouragement of her pastor which kept her from ending her life. Her deeply rooted beliefs, and being carried at that time by her God, gave her the power to uproot. She moved her five , ages two through twelve, reinventing herself by going to work as a full-time nurse. It was tough times for the five of us children. I had an older brother and sister and a younger brother and sister, and was lost somewhere in the middle. But my mom was always there for me, and for us, even when she could not always be there physically.

After my father's premature death due to alcoholism and heavy lifelong smoking, my oldest sister was able to courageously share with all of us the abuse she suffered at his hands. Our whole family began its slow healing from codependency and abuse through counseling, talking more openly, support groups like Adult Children of Alcoholics, more counseling, and hugs all around. Our ongoing family healing process has allowed all of us to share our love more openly with one another, and to listen better in regards to past struggles with our father and with each other.

Some years ago, after fifty years as a nurse, my mother retired. Though she was past the retirement age, she wanted to continue to use her healing gifts in caring for others, so she went back to school. She obtained a reflexology license and began massaging clients' feet for deep, holistic healing. She recently celebrated her eighty-sixth birthday and still sees a number of clients each week who are blessed by her healing touch. She is an open conduit of God's healing power though massage, listening, and if they are open to it, healing prayer.

My mother has always pushed me to do more by encouraging me to "go for it," whether that meant moving to the Hawaiian islands when I was seventeen, or taking my five-month dream trip to Europe at twenty-one. And she was right there for me when I was broken by my last drink, two and a half years ago, lying on the bottom and looking up. Just last evening, as I was yet unsure about my future, she told me I will do well whatever I do. Although I'm still growing up and don't know what the future holds, my mother has taught me through her faithful words and actions that even though we don't know what the future holds, God holds the future.

Thanks, Mom, for more than you know. Thank you for carrying me, both literally and in so many other ways. Happy Mother's Day!

Your loving and thankful recovery son, Ken.

P.S. Thank you for watching and waiting for me as you prayed, knowing that when this prodigal returned, I would be welcomed home with open arms!

Letting Go of a Loved One

I am learning about recovery from the inside out, learning about deep healing, abandonment issues, and letting go. I think about the ongoing losses in our lives, some of which are directly related to the consequences of our addictions. I think of the times I have attended a funeral for someone I did not know real well, but all the losses of those I've known so well have come flooding back over me.

Many years ago while serving my third-year internship from seminary at a huge church on the southeastern Gold Coast of Florida, I was visiting with my supervisor in his office when a young woman rushed in, crying loudly and wanting to talk to a clergy person. She told us that her fiancé had just been killed in a motorcycle accident. They had planned to be married the following month. My supervisor looked at me, and said, "Take over," and abandoned me!

There was little I could say to this grieving,

almost hysterical woman. I actually listened for over ninety minutes as she poured out her heart for her loved one. At the end, she said something I've never forgotten and have grown to understand more deeply in my recovery: "I am so thankful for the time we did have together, rather than being sad for the time we will never have together." I have often repeated this story and truth.

Life is a constant letting-go, but we only truly let go when we can take the very best of what we had with us. Our loved ones never die until we forget about them. A summary of these thoughts came to mind when I read the following poem from David Harkin:

You can shed tears that she is gone, or you can smile because she has lived.

You can close your eyes and pray that she'll come back, or you can open your eyes and see all she's left.

Your heart can be empty because you can't see her, or you can be full of the love you shared.

You can turn your back on tomorrow and live yesterday, or you can be happy for tomorrow because of yesterday.

You can remember her only that she is gone, or you can cherish her memory and let it live on.

You can cry and close your mind, be empty and turn your back. Or you can do what she'd want: smile, open your eyes, love and go on."

Not Missing the Mystery

I am not a human being trying to find a spiritual existence....I am a spiritual being living in a human existence.

The more I read and listen and study, trying not to think too much, the more I realize that all life is spiritual. "Stinking thinking" has always been a common phrase among those of us in recovery, but it's an across-the-board truth when we consider how our thoughts can control us, rather than our being still and letting go of our mental compulsions. I know from whence I speak regarding such compulsions—they are a bubbling spring within that often becomes a raging torrent!

I read a great line by the philosopher Blaise Pascal this week: *All the troubles of man come from his not knowing how to sit still.* Amazing! Think of how many mysteries we miss because we cannot sit still long enough for them to be revealed. This echoes well Psalm 46:10: *Be still and know that I am God.* On my more negative days, my inner voice says "Be busy and know that you are God, the master of your destiny and captain of your ship: you need not answer to anyone." Herein lies the blessedness of hitting bottom. When one is on his back looking up, or on his knees in prayer, this phrase rings true: "Get on your knees and fight like a man."

Therefore, if all is spiritual, each moment is a godly moment and something to be thankful for as an amazing gift, pregnant with possibilities. I am thankful that even though this is much easier to write than live, I am able to be in that *present* a little more often in the midst of my busy days, which increases my chances of not missing the mystery.

May the present mysteries surprise us and become ever more real in our daily recovery.

The Dizziness of Freedom

Anxiety is the dizziness of freedom.
—Soren Kierkegaard

My first thought upon reading this phrase from Kierkegaard was a flashback to the many years I spent visiting men in prisons and jails. Some of them would tell me that living on the outside was too much to handle—too much temptation for them to be able to consistently make the right choices.

Some of the inmates attending our small groups would say they felt safe and protected when locked up; others, having had a spiritual awakening, would say they are more free now in prison than they had ever been on the outside. These men were actually looking forward to their paroles so they could put their new, inner spiritual strength into practice. They believed their lives would not only be different, but much better.

We did not have to wait long to see the outer change that arose from their inner change. One inmate, after surrendering to his Higher Power, felt an inner conviction to confess to a crime he had committed but was never arrested for. We could not believe it. He had been meeting with our recovery group twice a month for almost a year. At the end of one meeting he said to all of us, "I've never told anyone about a crime I committed in Kansas, but after I finish my time here, I'm going there to confess it and serve whatever sentence is given me." And he did! I followed up on him through the prison chaplain. He actually went and served his time for his crime.

What a great witness to us all, resonating with one of AA's foundational truths: "To thine own self be true." Here was a living testimony, transforming the anxiety of too much freedom into that empowering freedom we receive to do the next right thing each day. "Get 'er done!" His walking the talk helped all of us continue to move beyond daily surviving to a lifetime of thriving, one day at a time.

Higher Power, thank you for the inner strength to be brutally honest with ourselves and others. Help us to practice what we preach and imitate what others do.

Wounded Healers

If someone asked me, "What is the most empowering and life-giving aspect of your recovery journey?" I could describe it with two words: *Wounded Healers*. Those words come from Henri Nouwen, an insightful Roman Catholic priest and extraordinary writer who was a conduit of God's light shining through his brokenness, freeing others to be the same. His famous recovery phrase is, "The walking wounded have become the wounded healers." This phrase is alive and never ceases to empower me.

There was a time after I hit bottom, crashing and burning, when I could be described as a veteran of foreign wars. My life wreaked of what I thought was tragedy beyond recovery. I knew in my mind that things would never be the same, but I did not know in my heart that things could actually be better! Now begins a new journey, a new recovery, a new life that is slowly growing better, even beyond what it used to be.

Despite this living proof and power, many people I come into contact with are still trying to swim to the surface for air. They are feeling trapped like a panicked swimmer caught beneath the thick winter ice with no hole to climb out of. Yet I can also laugh with others in the program who sometimes joke, "I know that through this amazing, healing 12-step program, the light I can clearly see at the end of that dark tunnel is *not* an oncoming train"! Even with all these amazing truths around me that are sometimes working through me, I am often unconvinced, trying instead to live life with my own limited, failing power. It is during these doubting, vulnerable times that I am sent to other wounded healers who reassure, comfort, and stay with me.

And why can't our wounded healers be God in the flesh, living in and flowing through the loved ones He sends around us? Their words of comfort and unconditional love heal us; they empower us to risk cracking the door and trusting once more by giving ourselves to another who will carry us. As they do, they too are given joy for their journey.

Lord, thank you for being the
wounded healer for me.

+ + +

221

Listen to the M.U.S.I.C.

The word *music* can be seen as an acronym, **M.U.S.I.C.**, which reminds me of my Higher Power and of the 12 Steps: **M**elodies **U**nknown **S**pecifically **I**n **C**onsciousness.

Perhaps there have been sacred songs inside us from the beginning, but we could not hear them; we were not tuned into them, as the frequencies were too sensitive for our base, non-recovery reception to pick up. This is not unlike the phrase describing a true friend: *One who is able to sing back to you the life songs you have forgotten.* (Certainly more in context than another questionable though funny phrase about a true friend: *"An acquaintance may perhaps bail you out of jail, but a true friend will be sitting in jail with you, saying, 'Damn, that was fun!'"*)

As the 12 Steps become ingrained in my being, I see them relating to so many things, including music. Here's a simple breakdown of the Steps in the context of our musical theme:

Steps 1-3: Plugging Into the MUSIC

Steps 4-9: Getting Rid of Poor Reception

Step 10: Daily Listening Better

Step 11: Hearing Musical Harmonies

Step 12: Helping Others Hear the Music

Thank you for sharing your amazing M.U.S.I.C with me and through me!

Step 12

*Having had a spiritual awakening
as the result of these Steps, we tried to carry
this message to alcoholics, and to practice
these principles in all our affairs.*

Theme: Service

Spiritual + Experiences

The topic of my AA meeting yesterday was "Spiritual Experiences." The chairperson wanted others to share stories about enlightening experiences they have had in their recovery. She went on to say, "If that is too much to share, a second topic can be sponsorship." The group found out at the end of the meeting that the reason she chose the topic was due to something spiritual she had experienced the week before and wanted to share it with us.

Most of the sharing during the meeting could be summarized as: "I've had a couple of things happen to me that might be called a spiritual experience, but the greatest experience for me is being sober today, which is a true miracle!" All agreed, even though many seemed to be hoping for bright lights, angel visitations, and audible voices telling them what to do next. A freeing expression came to my mind and I smiled: "Sometimes the most spiritual thing you can do for yourself is to get eight hours of sleep!"

For me, the most beautiful part of all the sharing was simply being reminded why I am here: To love God and to love others. Two members in particularly shared that in a powerful way. One woman said she felt like dirt at the lowest point of her using and kept crying out to God, asking why she was still here. Her Higher Power simply responded, because I love you. Then a guy shared that he had always wondered what his purpose in life was, until this past week. His friend was in a life-and-death situation. He prayed, and words came out of his mouth that were not his own which greatly helped his friend. Now he feels on top of the world. He went on to say: "My life is still messed up, but I know now why I am here—to help others!"

I thought to myself, "Yes, this is so simple! Why does the world make it so complicated and mysterious?" I think one answer to this question is that the truth of why we are here is so obvious that people either do not want to do it, or do not have the power to do it, so they make it complicated and beyond knowing. Why do we think we have to know a specific purpose for life or destiny or whatever, when the two greatest commandments are: 1) loving God (as we understand God); and 2) loving our neighbor as ourselves.

These are our vertical and horizontal relationships: we are empowered to reach up to the God of our understanding, and as we do, we are empowered to reach across to another. This action also forms a cross, one of the symbols of my Higher Power.

One member shared from her *Big Book* the spiritual story of Bill W., who graciously received a visit from an old friend whom he thought had been "committed for alcohol insanity." This friend called Bill up, came over, and sat with him at his kitchen table—a walking miracle! Bill writes:

But my friend sat before me, and he made the point-blank declaration that God had done for him what he could not do for himself. His human will had failed. Doctors had pronounced him incurable. Society was about to lock him up. Like myself, he had admitted complete defeat. Then he had, in effect, been raised from the dead, suddenly taken from the scrap heap to a level of life better than the best he had even known! That floored me. It began to look as though religious people were right after all. Here was something at work in a human heart which had done the impossible. My ideas about miracles were drastically revised right then. Never mind the musty past; here sat a miracle directly across the kitchen table. He shouted great tidings.

Fourth Edition, p. 11

Have You Heard the Popping Sound?

I walked into work on Tuesday where Lance, the day-shift Resident Assistant (RA), was working at the front desk. Lance is colorful. He is a very down-to-earth, Harley-riding, fixing-and-ratcheting kind of guy who often says the first thing that comes to mind and doesn't apologize for it. He is refreshing. Maybe an apt description of Lance would be "quietly spiritual and loudly profane," though that might be generous.

So, I said, "Hey, Lance, tonight's my first time presenting at an AA Speakers' meeting. Have you ever done that?" "Oh yeah," Lance replied, "many times--experience, strength, and hope." He went on for a while. I listened. Then he looked right at me and said with some seriousness, "Ken, have you heard the popping sound?" I didn't have a clue what he meant and was almost afraid to ask, but it didn't matter, he was going to tell me anyway. "Ken, that's when you finally take your head out of your ass and begin real recovery!"

Well OK! Thank you, Brother Lance! That helps me see things much more clearly! Thank you for clarifying my recovery status, no longer bent over in a contorted, using position.

As I began my talk that night in front of a very large group of hungry recovering addicts and alcoholics, I was surprised and a little unnerved to see a number of clients from where I work sitting in the front row, smiling at me, wondering, and waiting. I began by quoting the free wisdom Lance shared with me about the popping sound. That broke the ice; I was speaking their language, as many knew exactly what I was talking about. They demonstrated active listening with rapt attention and gave great feedback afterward. Some amazing coincidences surfaced after the meeting during our fellowship over cake and ice cream—people who knew people who knew me well. "It's a small (recovery) world after all."

"I have been enlightened! I have been to the mountain top, and I have heard the popping sound!" Though amusing, all of us in true recovery know what that means. When that sound is behind us, we can allow real recovery to wash over us. We can better step out in faith, being used to heal others. We witness everyday miracles that are no longer few and far between.

———————————

Here's to putting the popping sound behind us!

———————————

Prepare for Liftoff
Without Alcohol

A friend asked me the other day how I'm doing without drinking. It was almost like she was asking, "I can't believe you haven't drunk or been tempted to drink! How is that possible? How are you really doing this?" What this person was saying to me between the lines was "You know, Ken, I like to drink wine, though I know it causes some problems in my life, but I don't think I could just give it up as you seem to be doing." I felt it was *that* kind of questioning, which reminded me of what someone said in a meeting the week before: ***"There's nothing in my life so bad that alcohol can't make it worse!"*** The most important thing about my own personal growth in recovery is that I finally understand this—it resonates deep within me.

Life is difficult enough without my pouring fuel on the fires of my daily, now manageable struggles. It is hard enough keeping some kind of balance. I feel I am walking a tightrope between work and school; this has been going on so long I'm not even sure what real balance is any more. It is amazing grace alone that gives me the strength and desire each day to continue to grow in my recovery. Perhaps the phrase *delicate balance* fits well; how smart would it be to take this delicate balance, this very sensitive and easily destroyed ecosystem of my recovery and pour gallons of alcohol into it? My thoughts exactly.

Just because I don't drink doesn't make everything good, but it certainly doesn't make them any worse. It gives me a healthy launch pad from which to blast off. Perhaps blasting off is too ambitious a phrase for my current feelings and situation, as my launches have been scrubbed quite a few times. But at least I'm cleared for liftoff! It's a go, because I'm clean and sober today!

+ + +

Reaching Out

Reaching out is a descriptive foundational phrase for my recovery today. I am reaching out to my Higher Power, to others, and to myself, all combined in one. It's good not to leave *myself* out of my recovery, and today will be filled with all of this: with class, learning to better listen to others' stories, along with two AA meetings and a sponsee meeting. God will be doing for me this day what I cannot do for myself. As I write these words, I remember I signed up last month to lead the topic at both of today's meetings. Well, at least I know what the topic will be.

I cannot reach *out* if I can't first reach *up*! On my own, I have no strength or desire or will or anything. Because of my own powerlessness, amazing grace comes to help me reach up so I can reach out to others, sharing the message. I was that drowning man, going under for the last time, when that unconditional love threw me the eternal life preserver. Life can throw me an anchor, but my Higher Power throws me a Life preserver: my life is preserved so I can assist in the rescue of others.

In looking back over my entire life, with all my struggles and all my successes, I think about the creation story of Genesis. I was dust, created from the earth, and it was not until my Higher Power breathed into me that I became a living soul. Fast-forward to my recovery. Without that connection, that breathing into me on a daily basis by my Higher Power, I do not have the desire to desire it. Without that power—that infusion—I believe I'm powerless not only over alcohol, but also to reach out to my Higher Power. This is *grace*. This is where God as I understand God shines the brightest. This power is a deep, spiritual love; ONE that first loved me. I receive that love that cannot be contained—it overflows and is further multiplied as I give it away.

This truth is extremely simple, powerful, and life-giving. It takes the *me* away from trying to be God. It beckons me daily to come and rest in the everlasting arms. I am inwardly reminded to continue to say *yes* to the voice within, and to grow in discerning and deciphering it more clearly.

An intern in class yesterday shared her understanding of the cross, since another classmate had challenged her with his own perception of it. She said a helpful image for her has been the picture of a person standing tall and straight with both arms stretched out in the form of a cross. With one arm she reaches back, taking hold of past blessings that empowered her; with the other arm she reaches forward to the person in need, regardless of what they believe or don't believe. She can only do this because her feet are firmly planted in the present. I like that; I am strengthened by that.

Blessings to us all on this recovery day,
keeping our feet firmly planted in the life-giving
soil of unconditional love, pushing us forward to
reach out to another, just as others have
reached back to us.

October 14, 2010

My Guilt-Free Tuesday
My Guilt-Free Life

Today I am celebrating four years of active sobriety. To best celebrate, I was able to get someone to work for me, and will spend the next twelve hours doing nothing or doing anything; most importantly, I choose this day to be guilt-free. Free from the small stuff of not having to do things around the house in order to feel like my day is worth something, free from the big stuff of not pressuring myself to pursue a better-paying job that is more life-giving and better suited to my gifts and talents. I have done all that and more, and need to continue to let go and let God—He knows my address, and He is helping me to hear his daily knocking a little more clearly.

I am spending the day going inward, so to speak. After doing my morning exercises at a relaxed pace, not pushing myself, I spent twenty minutes in simple meditation, calming my breathing and my mind and achieving a relaxation bordering on sleep. Nice (and why am I not doing this more often?). After writing these words I will spend forty-five minutes with an amazing guided-imagery CD my mother gave me that helps deal with letting go of past hurts and pain through a variety of losses, using soothing words of spiritual light and counsel. This is my four-year sober birthday, my **G**uilt **F**ree **T**uesday, GFT, or better-stated: **GIFT!** My gift to myself, and thereby to others around me.

Therefore, it begs the question: If I can set aside a Guilt Free Day," why can't I set aside a "Guilt Free Life"? The simple answer is, "I AM!" I am doing this, or better yet, the I AM is doing this in me through my transformational recovery program; hence the opening phrase: *four years of active sobriety."* A better answer, THE ANSWER for me and so many millions in active sobriety is:

The I AM, the Spiritual nature of God as we understand God, living in and through our lives, is assisting and empowering us to not merely survive but to also thrive.

I interpret active sobriety with the 12 Steps and specifically Step 12:

Having had a spiritual awakening as a result of these steps, we tried to carry the message to other alcoholics, and to practice these principles in all our affairs.

Active sobriety means to be fully involved and integrated into the program of AA. For me this includes weekly meetings, meeting with my sponsor and sponsees, daily readings and reflecting on recovery literature, and being woven into the fabric of service work (treasurer, medallions, preparing coffee, setup, and so on). It becomes a way of life. And perhaps the most obvious sign of active sobriety is that I am available when someone else in recovery is in need...at least I am growing in being more available.

Yes, a way of life—a growing guilt-free life based on a growing number of guilt-free days.

Celebrating Five Years' Sobriety

One Guilt-Free day at a Time!
(...And This Book's Final Entry)

October 14, 2011

I had planned on ending this book with my last entry celebrating four years of sobriety, but it's been another year of life-changing recovery and continual work on finishing this manuscript. This coming week I'll be receiving my five-year medallion, presented to me by my loving wife of thirty-four years and my amazing sponsor who has thirty-nine years' sobriety. But this is not the reason for this final post.

There is an incident in my life and recovery that refuses to let me go and needs to be shared. It hit me last month that for some reason I had never included it, and I think that reason had to do with shame and pain and burying the event, despite its powerful teaching value. The reason it surfaced so strongly this week was due to the second relapse in the past few months of one of my sponsees. He had just graduated from his second treatment in the past year, only to abuse alcohol last week while driving, receiving a DUI and spending the night in jail. Other immediate consequences will include receiving the big whiskey "W" on his license plates, having the in car breathalyzer hook up in order to start his car, and he will still face the wrath of the judge in court in the near future.

In recovery we are not here to judge or condemn another, not only because we are that person, having been where they have been, but also because we can encourage the other and continue to grow ourselves by sharing our stories: who we are, what happened and how we've changed for the better because of it. That discussion surfaced as my guilt-ridden and shamed sponsee called me the day after being pulled over.

As we visited together on the phone, the only thing I could share with him was similarly insane behavior one month before my almost fatal motorcycle accident and my shameful hitting bottom over five years ago. I remember it was an extremely hot summer day, almost one hundred degrees, and I had forced an argument with my wife so I could have an excuse to get angry enough to hop on my motorcycle and drive north seven hours, crossing the border into Thunder Bay, Manitoba, Canada.

A few hours north of St. Cloud I bought a twelve-pack and drank a few along the way. I got to Grand Marais and had a couple more. It was starting to lightly rain and it was going to be dark in an hour or so, but I thought, "I know, I'll find one of my pottery friends who live along Lake Superior just a half hour away. I'm sure I can stay there for a while and maybe even overnight." I decided not to wear a helmet.

I had forgotten exactly where my friend lived but I knew it was off a sandy side road toward the shore of Lake Superior. It was beginning to thunder now, raining harder. The alcohol was buzzing in my head and my visibility was being impaired, especially as I tried to navigate the narrow paths. I remember a tree branch hitting me in the face and my front tire going off the path, and I came crashing down into a deep ditch. I was pinned under my huge motorcycle, though I didn't feel I was injured. I looked two feet to the right of my head and realized I had just missed a huge boulder. It was now beginning to lightning and thunder loudly. As I laid on my back with my face in the air and the rain just pummeling me, I had to almost laugh out loud, a crazy fearful laugh, thinking, *"This is such a classic image of the worst of my crazy drinking!"* Though it could have been much worse!

I finally managed to pull my right foot out of my motorcycle boot, get out and walk to the nearest cabin. I knocked on the door, but no one was home. I got to the next lake home and a nice couple answered the door, took one look at me and said, "Wow, you look like you could use a beer!!" Even then I said, "That would be great!" *Crazy!* I spent the next couple hours at their home while the husband called his towing service friend, who couldn't come out until morning.

I could tell this helpful neighbor was not about to invite me to stay the night at his home, but he did say he'd drive me to the Grand Portage Casino nearby. All the rooms were booked and there was nowhere else to stay, so I played some games slowly for hours and tried to sleep on the beach; the mosquitoes would not let me rest.

The next morning the tow truck drove the thirty-plus miles out from Grand Marais. The driver took one look at my motorcycle lying seven feet below us in the ditch, and said, "You know, even if I can get it out, and assuming it's not damaged, I don't think there's any way it's gonna start!" He expertly attached the wide straps onto it and hoisted it right out. There was only one small crack in the corner of the windshield. The rest of the bike was in great shape. Amazing! I turned the key and it started right up. I gave him my Visa card and the rescue was complete...but it was really just beginning.

There was a battle already raging in my head and heart. I drove my motorcycle slowly down the long driveway. I looked to the left and wondered if I should just drive home to St. Cloud, to my family and friends and work—the sane choice—or turn right and go north to Thunder Bay, the insane choice. I chose the latter. I spent all that night drinking in a small hotel room, got up the next morning before sunrise and drove home. After only an hour's driving I almost passed out on my bike, shaking and realizing I had drunk no fluids other than alcohol for the past twenty-four hours and was becoming severely dehydrated. I managed to get to a small restaurant and replenish my fluids, gaining enough strength to drive the next leg of the trip, stopping, and doing the same until I got home.

In my alcoholic thinking and judgment, I decided *not* to do the right thing. Even though I was rescued and miraculously delivered from a potentially life-threatening accident, and even after my motorcycle survived in great shape, I *still* didn't get it! One month later I had my horrific accident that landed me in the hospital, in the papers, in treatment, in a year of recovery, and in a total life change of shame and pain.

But God does not judge us, He rescues us. He gives us many opportunities for healing whether we accept them or not. We keep running away and, I believe, He needs to work in greater ways to get our attention. He never gives up on us and holds us close, even as we are bleeding and injured in so many ways. But he does work through ALL THINGS for the good, though perhaps more for our eternal good.

But today, after five years of active sobriety through living the program, attending weekly meetings, and sharing my recovery in every way possible with everyone I come into contact with, it's true: *My worst day has become my best day!* My Higher Power is not interested in putting me back together again, like some Humpty-Dumpty cracked egg! I am becoming a brand new creation, more than I have ever been, as nothing is wasted, everything is recycled and *all things are made new.*

This is what I shared with my friend on the phone. This is one of his worst days, but, by the grace of God, as he understands God, it also can become his best day, regardless of how many times he has squandered his wealth on riotous living. His loving God is always waiting with outstretched arms for him to come home—no questions asked; no condemnation, only a deep reservoir of love and acceptance and a glimmer of light that helps my friend know that he is now being carried.

Soli Deo Gloria
To God Alone Be The Glory

Bibliography

Thanks to the publishers for permission to excerpt from the following published works:

Mark Nepo, *The Book of Awakening,* (Conari Press, an imprint of Wheel/Weiser LLC, 2000).

Philip Parham, *Letting God,* (Harper One, an imprint of HarperCollins, 1987).

The Hazelden Foundation, *Twenty-Four Hours A Day* (Center City, MN: Hazelden Foundation 1996).

Corrie ten Boom, excerpted from "I'm Still Learning to Forgive" From *Guideposts* Magazine, Copyright © 1972 by Guideposts Associates, Inc., Carmel, New York, 10512.

The *Twelve Steps* are reprinted and adapted with permission of *Alcoholics Anonymous World Services, Inc.* Permission to reprint and adapt the *Twelve Steps* does not mean that *AA* has reviewed or approved the contents of this publication, nor that *AA* agrees with the views expressed herein. *AA* is a program of recovery from alcoholism—use of the *Twelve Steps* in connection with programs and activities which are patterned after *AA*, but which address other problems, does not imply otherwise.

About The Author

I am fifty-eight years old, married for thirty-five years to Joan, an amazing and beautiful wife who has also grown tremendously in her own Al-Anon program. We have two grown, married children, one granddaughter, and a soon to be born grandson. We have lived in St. Cloud, MN for twenty-seven years. I served as a full-time church planter and parish pastor of the Lutheran Church-Missouri Synod for twenty-five years until I resigned in 2006 to pursue Hospital Chaplaincy in the St. Cloud area. I left that church body—and that world view—over five years ago through my own recovery, finding healing Spirituality rather than repressive Religion. I have grown in my understanding that all world religions contain the deep, healing truths incorporated in the 12 Steps of AA, drawn from the Bible and other sacred writings. I am also an artist of ceramic sculpture, wheel thrown and altered creations. I currently work with men in recovery through the St. Cloud Hospital, as well as serving as the Protestant Pastor, conducting Sunday Worship Services at Country Manor Campus, Sartell, MN.

Special Thanks

I personally want to thank my Higher Power—God as I understand God—for directing my life and thereby the contents of this book each step of the way. While these words came into existence out of my need to heal and make sense of my own tragic events from alcohol, it soon took on a recovery life of its' own, fueled by the walking miracles who have attended my weekly recovery meetings over the past five years.

This book and my recovery life would not have been possible without the amazing, unconditional love and support of my wife Joan. It was she who said through tears, while visiting me in treatment during our group family sessions, "I am willing to go through this pain now if it will make for a stronger marriage later." And as we celebrate our 35th wedding anniversary, alcohol free and thriving, it has made a deep, life-changing difference. Joan also became my 'Lay-Out Editor' in the second proof edit of this book, adding her special cognitive and artistic touches that assist in its' readability and enjoyment.

I also thank God for my loving and supportive two adult children and their wonderful spouses, my four brothers and sisters and their spouses, my ever prayerful and deeply supportive mother, and my always encouraging mother in law. All of them have been foundational, far beyond what words can describe, in helping me 'go the distance' in this literary creation.

I also owe deep thanks to my amazing sponsor Ellis, who this year celebrated his 81st birthday and his 40th year of sobriety. Ellis is a friend, a brother in Christ, a healthy father-figure and someone who knows more about my life and struggles than anyone but God. He frees me up to weekly sit and share and laugh and talk about anything and everything.

A special part of this book are also the many sponsees I have been able to help along the way as they have helped me—we are all woven together in a healing, recovery tapestry.

Finally, the completion of this book would be impossible without so many of you who have shared your love and support from weekly meetings to half way around the world on special recovery sites giving and receiving feedback on blogs and recovery topics—you know who you are! These pages grew out of those creative, informative, and challenging exchanges...

...Yes, To God Be The Glory!

Made in the USA
Monee, IL
28 March 2020